How to Be Blessed

How to Be
Blessed

Unless otherwise indicated,
all Scripture quotations are taken from
the Holy Bible, King James Version.

How to Be Blessed
Copyright © 2001 by Orman Press, Inc.

ISBN: 1-891773-27-5

Printed in the United States of America

Table of Contents

Dedication

I dedicate this book to the blessed family of the McCalep's of this generation and future generations.

First, to my blessed wife, Dr. Sadie McCalep, who God blessed me with at a pivotal point in my life and who has experienced the entire "from a little to much" blessed journey with me.

Also, to my three handsome, blessed sons, Michael Orman, George Orman III, and Timothy Orman, and one grandson, Christopher Orman, all who represent my crowned favor from God, as well as the only hope for the future perpetuation of the name God has blessed—McCalep.

Foreword

Dr. George O. McCalep has written with clarity, conviction, and in a conversational tone. One can almost "hear" the words as they are read. He brings to bear his own insights on a theme that has received much attention lately—the relationship between human faithfulness to God's commands and the resultant of divine favors. Dr. McCalep's theological position prompts the reader to a personal, critical and honest exploration of the total biblical message on the subject. If material blessings are a sign of the believer's accessing of divine resources through "asking" and "faithfulness," then is the absence of abundant blessing a judgment of God for unfaithfulness? Sober theological pondering is in order. I commend Dr. McCalep's book as a stimulating contribution of engagement in this theological probing.

Introduction

What is a blessing? I think sometimes we get blessings mixed up with other things, like presents. You can go to a store and buy a present, but you can't go to a store and buy a blessing from God. God gives you a talent when you are born. Sometimes you are born with an innate ability for athleticism or for music. But a blessing is even more than that. A blessing comes from the sovereign God who gives undeservedly to whom He wants, whenever He wants, however He wants.

How to Be Blessed is a biblical guide to being blessed according to God's Word. It is based on the biblical truth that God promised to bless His obedient children. The operative word here is "obedient." God loves us unconditionally, but most of His biblical blessing promises come with a condition. There is some fine print in God's contracts. In secular contracts, often the fine print is deceptively positioned and hidden.

Unlike secular contracts, God does not hide the fine print, we just choose to ignore it. We want the blessing without the conditions. We want the crown without the cross. We want the joy of the resurrection without the suffering of the crucifixion. We want Easter Sunday without Good Friday.

How to Be Blessed guides you in the path to be blessed by the way of the cross. How to Be Blessed is not based on what has been labeled "prosperity Gospel." However, there is a fine line of demarcation between prosperity gospel and the promise of God that He wants His children to prosper. The fine line is generally found in the fine print of obedience, dependence on Him, and temporary circumstances or conditions. God has not cursed people who are poor in material wealth. As a matter of truth, biblically speaking, God has always found special favor with the oppressed, the least and the unlikely. From this truth, we get a biblical, theological foundation for a liberation gospel.

Liberation gospel and prosperity gospel are only in conflict when either or both are given to extremes. We must remember, the result of liberation is freedom. Freedom for what? Freedom to be all that God would have us to be. Freedom to prosper spiritually and materially. Resurrections do follow crucifixions. Joy does come in the morning. There is a crown after the cross. There is a bright side somewhere, and there is a blessing on the other side of through. *How to Be Blessed* is a guide to help believers receive the blessings on the other side of through without ignoring the "through." In other words, without ignoring the way of the cross.

More Than a Sneeze

In Bruce Wilkinson's book entitled *The Prayer of Jabez*, he states that "blessing is not about sneezing" because the end result of being blessed is piles of blessings.[1] I concur indeed that to be truly blessed is much more than a sneeze. A common expression said after someone sneezes, is "bless you." Taken seriously, a "bless you" response to a sneeze dilutes the true biblical meaning of the word and the concept of being blessed. *How to Be Blessed* is about more than a "bless you" response to a sneeze. *How to Be Blessed* is about a lifestyle that will result in a life marked by one blessing after another on a continuous basis. Blessings will follow us, and blessings will run interference in front of us. To be blessed according to the Bible means to be the recipient of a supernatural favor that ultimately could only have been initiated by God. A favor that neither we nor any other human could have done. A favor that could not have been obtained by any self-doing or human endeavor. Biblically speaking, we cannot bless ourselves, but God can make us a blessing. We can become a blessing for God and a blessing on behalf of God, but ultimately all blessings come from and are initiated by God. As you continue to read *How to Be Blessed*, prepare yourself to begin a journey stamped by supernatural favor (miracles) and not "bless you" responses from an allergic sneeze. Remember that God wants to bless. It is His nature to bless. He is a blessing God who takes pleasure in blessing. Read *How to Be Blessed* with an open, obedient spirit and prepare to be showered with blessings.

How to Be Blessed is not only about finding favor with God but also man. Why man? Why not only finding favor with God? Impossible! When we find favor with God, we automatically find favor with man. Finding favor with God guarantees favor with others. God works in mysterious ways, including blessing us through others. God uses human agencies as well as situations and circumstances to bless. As we will discuss in the following chapters, God promises us through the promises given to Abraham, not only to bless us, but also to make us a blessing. He also promises to bless or curse others depending on whether they bless us. There is a relationship between finding favor with God and finding favor with man. In addition, we are reminded that Jesus grew in favor with God and man. *"And Jesus increased in wisdom and stature, and in favour with God and man."* (Luke 2:52 - KJV) It is our ultimate goal to be like Jesus. Be blessed by reading *How to Be Blessed* and find favor with God and man.

Presupposition to Being Blessed

Webster defines a presupposition as an antecedent to logic or fact. Simply put, it is something that is supposed to happen before something else occurs. *How to Be Blessed* presupposes that the reader is a believer who has potential to be blessed. If you are not a believer and want to be blessed, I invite you right now to believe in and put your faith in Jesus Christ as Lord. To be the beneficiary of the truths and principles espoused in this book, the reader must be a believer. The Bible asserts in Mark 11:22–24 (KJV): *"And Jesus answering saith unto them, Have faith in God. For verily I say unto you, That whosoever shall say unto this mountain, Be thou removed, and be thou cast into the sea; and shall not doubt in his heart, but shall believe that those things which he saith shall come to pass; he shall have whatsoever he saith. Therefore I say unto you,*

What things soever ye desire, when ye pray, believe that ye receive them, and ye shall have them."

In order to be blessed we must be able to see with the eyes of faith and believe in our hearts that God is able to perform according to His promises. If you can concur and believe, you can receive. *How to Be Blessed* presupposes that you have faith in God to be motivated to keep the condition in God's covenant promises to bless.

Asking—A Key Factor to Being Blessed

". . . We have not because we ask not" (James 4:2 - KJV). Hide this scripture in your heart, make it a part of your constant thinking and you will be blessed. Asking is the most simple and obvious, yet the most underused, ignored, and neglected factor in being blessed. Why? Because we have not yet fully internalized that it is the nature of God to bless, and we cannot spiritualize in our understanding the unlimited wealth of God. We cannot conceive that we have a generous, extravagant Father with unlimited blessings. We seem to think that because He has blessed us once, and He blessed our friends and relatives, that He must be running short or running out of blessings. God's blessings are unlimited. If we keep on asking over and over again, then He

will keep on blessing over and over again. We seem to think that we worry God when we keep asking and that because He blessed us once, He does not want to hear from us again. Also, we are so pious in our praying that we feel we are selfish if we keep asking God continuously for blessings. God is like any loving parent who wants his children to have all that he has for them and who enjoys the relationship that takes place in the asking. Matthew 7:7–11(KJV) gives us some insight into God's parenting nature.

> *"Ask, and it shall be given you; seek, and ye shall find; knock, and it shall be opened unto you: For every one that asketh receiveth; and he that seeketh findeth; and to him that knocketh it shall be opened. Or what man is there of you, whom if his son ask bread, will he give him a stone? Or if he ask a fish, will he give him a serpent? If ye then, being evil, know how to give good gifts unto your children, how much more shall your Father which is in heaven give good things to them that ask him?"*

Jesus admonishes us over and over again to ask! Notice, the conditions of *abiding* and *asking* in His name.

*"And whatsoever ye shall ask in my name,
that will I do, that the Father may be glorified
in the Son. If ye shall ask any thing in my
name, I will do it (John 14:13–14 - KJV).*

*"If ye abide in me, and my words abide in
you, ye shall ask what ye will, and it shall be
done unto you"(John 15:7- KJV).*

I believe that God would not repeatedly tell us to ask if He did not want us to ask repeatedly. We shouldn't hesitate to make asking a constant point in our prayers. We should ask God over and over again to bless us. How would we feel if when we get to heaven and Peter, the keeper of the gate, took us on a tour and showed us all of the unclaimed blessings, including the ones that had our names on them? There are many blessings that don't get claimed because we simply fail to ask. How many times have we been blessed with blessings for which we did not ask? Well, they are only a fraction of the blessings that have our names on them; we must ask for the others. Remember, one of the key factors in being blessed is knowing who we want to become in Christ and having the courage to ask for it. If you decide not to read any more of this book, turn immediately to the last chapter and accept the personal challenge to participate in the formula that will assure you that your life will be blessed. Don't deny the blessings that belong to you.

Testimony

I consider myself to be a blessed man. How am I blessed? I am both spiritually and financially blessed. I am also blessed to love others: those whom God has given me, those who are believers and those who are not. I am also blessed by the rain that falls in my life. Lastly, I am blessed to be loosed to serve God. I am indeed a blessed man.

Spiritually Blessed

I define "spiritually blessed" as being set free from the bondage of anger, hate, lust, fear, drugs, pride and materialism. God set me free from the penalty of sin when, in Christ, He died on the cross and by the power of the resurrection He delivered me from all of the above. Therefore, I consider myself spiritually wealthy—in Christ. By His grace I have grown up in Christ to the point where I realize that spiritual blessings are superior to material blessings because spiritual blessings are everlasting, whereas material blessings are at best temporary. In addition, only those who are in Christ possess spiritual blessings.

In another book that I was blessed to write entitled *Growing Up to the Head: Ten Growth Essentials to Becoming a Better Christian,* I expound and list what I call a seven-fold doxology of spiritual blessings found in Ephesians 1:3—14:2. They are as follows:

Spiritual Blessing One: The joy of being chosen (v. 4)

Spiritual Blessing Two: The joy of adoption (v. 5–6)

Spiritual Blessing Three: The joy of redemption (v. 7)

Spiritual Blessing Four: The joy of wisdom (v. 8)

Spiritual Blessing Five: The joy of knowing (v. 9)

Spiritual Blessing Six: The joy of inheritance (v. 11)

Spiritual Blessing Seven: The joy of being sealed (v. 13–14)

All these spiritual blessings are given only to those who are in Christ. Nonbelievers are not blessed with these spiritual blessings. Therefore, as a believer, in Christ, I am especially blessed.

Materially and Financially Blessed

I also consider myself materially and financially blessed. My testimony is a poverty to prosperity journey. When my wife and I began our journey, we had absolutely nothing but a dim sense of the power of

God, love for each other, a desire to prosper and a desire to help others prosper. Our plans to accomplish this desire were through the implementation of a simple investment concept. We were obsessed with the idea of getting rich; we fell as victims to the evil spirit of materialism. God was not number one in our lives. God dealt with us mercifully by cutting us back to nearly zero financially so that He could deliver us from the bondage of materialism.

God's discipline blessed us during those critical years to discover that the secret to successful wealth building was to honor and obey Him. We learned to pay God first, thereby making Him an active partner in our business affairs and all other endeavors. We learned to pay ourselves second with a commitment to never spend the principle, compounded interest or appreciation unless it was an emergency. Therefore, we always lived on no more than 80 percent of our income. I believe that anyone following this simple formula and the biblical principles set forth in this book will be blessed by God.

I define being materially blessed as possessing all of the amenities of life that my heart desires. I am sure there are many other material things that could be possessed, but I have no desire to own them. I am blessed to have all the material things my heart desires. I do not have everything, but I have all I want. Many people have much more than I, but I have all my heart desires. Truly, I am blessed.

I define financially blessed as being financially independent. In other words, if I decided not to work for a living I would be able to maintain all that my heart desires. However, I do not plan to quit working until my health fails or God tells me to stop. I love my work, and to love your work is a blessing. To wake up every morning without an alarm clock and with a great expectation and anticipation of the joy of the workday is a blessing. I believe that I am doing exactly what God would have me to do, and I am using the talents and spiritual gifts He has given me to do it. I plan to use these gifts until the day I die, unless of course, God says something different. I am a blessed man. I have discovered that we cannot want to be more and do more for God without being financially and materially blessed. We should not try to be paupers for God. We should not deny the blessings. If we become more for God and do more for God, He is going to bless us materially and financially. There is nothing we can do about it, except of course bless others with our blessing, which only keeps more blessings coming. This is a part of the divine plan.

Blessed to Love Others

I love God first with all my heart, soul and mind. I love my wife, of 40 years, with all my heart and would be more than willing to die for her as Christ did the church. I love my children and their families, and it is my heart's desire that they would prosper both spiritually and materially. I love church. There is no place I'd rather be than with my family or in church. I pastor a loving church that is free of animosity and that I love very much. The membership clearly demonstrates its love for me and for my family.

I am also blessed to love people. I especially enjoy meeting and fellow worshipping with God's people all over this country. But I am also blessed to love the world and people of the world. Yes, I love unsaved people and even people who may not treat me right. *"For God so loved the world, that he gave his only begotten Son, that whosoever believeth in him should not perish, but have everlasting life"* (John 3:16 - KJV). How blessed I am to be blessed by the grace of God to love the world as Christ loved the world.

Blessed by the Rain

Yet, I am not so naive or unscripturally based as not to realize that *"it rains on the just and the unjust"*

(Matthew 5:45 - KJV). There are burdens in my life and it often rains on my parade.

I have had many challenges in my life. There have been and still are family challenges, yet I am still blessed. My mother died when I was four years old. Due in part to my old rebellious nature, my deceased stepmother and I were not always in a harmonious relationship. I was blessed to reconcile that relationship before she died. I have a son who carries my namesake who is challenged with a 99.9 percent hearing impairment. I am a healed alcoholic. My chemical allergic reaction to alcohol represents my thorn in the flesh. I realize that I may be one teaspoon of cough syrup away from being a person who cannot manage his life.

Blessed by Being Loosed

I understand and spiritualize my life to be blessed like the donkey Jesus rode on when He made His triumphant entry into Jerusalem on Palm Sunday. The donkey was loosed by the prophetical, providential power of God because the Lord had need of him saying, "*Go ye into the village over against you; in the which at your entering ye shall find a colt tied, whereon yet never man sat: loose him, and bring him hither. And if any man ask you, Why do ye loose him? thus shall ye say unto him, Because the Lord hath need of him."* (Luke 19:30–31 - KJV)

I am blessed because God loosed me to be used by Him. In addition, no one ever would have heard of that donkey if Jesus had not sat on him. Likewise, no one would have heard of me if God had not chosen to sit on me with an anointing to find favor with God and man.

Blessed to Write This Book

I am fully aware that material blessings are temporal and may be gone tomorrow. They came from God, belong to God, and may at any time be removed from my stewardship. But in the meantime I commit to being a good and faithful steward over the material and financial prosperity with which I have been blessed. All glory and honor belong to God. No flesh should ever glory in His presence. I simply thank God for allowing me to find favor with both Him and man.

I was inspired to write this book from the encouragement and requests of many who have seen the anointing of God's and man's favor on my life. The many include the congregation I serve and the majority of the deacons, particularly Deacon Gary McGaha.

How to Be Blessed is written to bless others. God has told me more than once to write what I give you—be blessed and bless others.

How to Be Blessed will take you on a biblical journey through messages designed to highlight the fine print in God's promises to bless His children. As you travel through these scripturally-based chapters, be obedient to the fine print and you will be blessed. Participating in the spiritual lessons taught in *How to Be Blessed* will protect you from the travesty of getting to heaven and having God show you all the blessings that bear your name that you refused to claim.

NOTES

1. *The Prayer of Jabez* - Bruce Wilkinson, p. 23
2. *Growing Up to the Head*, pp. 39–45

Blessed Through Harkening to His Voice

Deuteronomy 28:1–14 (KJV)

1 And it shall come to pass, if thou shalt hearken diligently unto the voice of the LORD thy God, to observe and to do all his commandments which I command thee this day, that the LORD thy God will set thee on high above all nations of the earth:

2 And all these blessings shall come on thee, and overtake thee, if thou shalt hearken unto the voice of the LORD thy God.

3 Blessed shalt thou be in the city, and blessed shalt thou be in the field.

4 Blessed shall be the fruit of thy body, and the fruit of thy ground, and the fruit of thy cattle, the *increase of thy kine, and the flocks of thy sheep.*

5 Blessed shall be thy basket and thy store.

6 Blessed shalt thou be when thou comest in, and blessed shalt thou be when thou goest out.

7 The LORD shall cause thine enemies that rise up against thee to be smitten before thy face: they shall come out against thee one way, and flee before thee seven ways.

8 The LORD shall command the blessing upon thee in thy storehouses, and in all that thou settest thine hand unto; and he shall bless thee in the land which the LORD thy God giveth thee.

9 The LORD shall establish thee an holy people unto himself, as he hath sworn unto thee, if thou shalt keep the commandments of the LORD thy God, and walk in his ways.

10 And all people of the earth shall see that thou art called by the name of the LORD; and they shall be afraid of thee.

11 And the LORD shall make thee plenteous in goods, in the fruit of thy body, and in the fruit of thy cattle, and in the fruit of thy ground, in the land which the LORD sware unto thy fathers to give thee.

12 The LORD shall open unto thee his good treasure, the heaven to give the rain unto thy land in his season, and to bless all the work of thine hand: and thou shalt lend unto many nations, and thou shalt not borrow.

13 And the Lord shall make thee the head, and not the tail; and thou shalt be above only, and thou shalt not be beneath; if that thou hearken unto the commandments of the LORD thy God, which I command thee this day, to observe and to do them:

14 *And thou shalt not go aside from any of the words which I command thee this day, to the right hand, or to the left, to go after other gods to serve them.*

God has promised that if we hearken diligently, He will bless us in powerful ways. God wants us to hear Him and do His will. God is a promise-keeper, and He has signed a contract to bless us. However, a word of caution is needed. We must not forget to read the fine print. Hearing must also be followed by doing. The word "hear" in the Bible means "do." Hearing means doing. Hearkening to His voice means keeping His commandments. If we hearken to His voice, we will be blessed.

> *Hearing means doing. Hearkening to His voice means keeping His commandments.*

Old Testament Lesson

The Old Testament scripture reference is from the book of Deuteronomy and is called the Second Law. It was written by Moses. It is the last book in the Pentateuch, the first five books of the Bible. It was written after the exodus experience, but before the Promised Land experience. This text was written after the Red Sea experience, but before the crossing of the Jordan River experience. God had led his people out of bondage. God led His people out of bondage in Egypt with one plague after another until the tenth plague where the death angel came over the houses and the firstborn was smitten. But God told Moses to tell the people to take the blood from an unblemished lamb and some hyssop and paint the blood on their doorposts so that when the death angel saw the blood, he would pass over. Jesus Christ is our Passover. If we are washed in the blood of the Lamb, when the death angel comes into our room, and sees the blood, then we will be passed over into eternal life.

However, we can work in a soap factory and still be dirty. The only way we can be clean is to wash with the soap. We can sit in a church with born-again believers, sing about the blood, talk about the blood, shout about the blood, but unless we have been washed in the blood, and unless the blood has been applied to our lives, we will still be dirty.

Moses had guided God's people for nearly forty years. Now Moses is of some age and God says to him, give them the Law one more time. So, old man Moses stands up and says one more time, "I want to tell you it shall come to pass that if thou shall harken diligently unto the voice of God and observe all these commandments, God will bless you. He will bless your coming in and your going out. He will bless you so you won't ever be the tail, you will always be the head. He will bless you so that blessings will even overtake you. God says if you hearken diligently, I will bless you in a very, very special way."

He will bless your coming in and your going out. He will bless you so you won't ever be the tail, you will always be the head.

Let us examine this covenant, promissory contract. Anytime anybody gives us a contract we should to read it carefully. As we read this covenant, promissory contract carefully, let us make sure we read the fine print.

God Can Bless Anywhere

First, look at what God says in verse 3. He says that I will bless you wherever you are. I will bless you in the city, and I will bless you in the field. God can bless you wherever your place is. He can bless you on the job or in school; He can bless you walking down the street or riding in a car or on a bicycle. He can bless you in your church or any other church. We do not have to be in a certain church to be blessed. People even mistakenly name their churches as the source of their blessings. We do not have to be under a certain pastor to be blessed. God is the Blesser. He can bless any church, anywhere. He will bless a church in the suburbs or in the country. We can be blessed in the inner city or on the farm. We can be blessed in the field or on any continent, or in any country. God is a blessing God and He says that we do not have to be in a certain place to be blessed. He will bless us where we are. Make sure you are in your place, whether it's downtown or uptown or midtown.

We do not have to be in a certain church to be blessed.

God Will Bless Our Efforts

God will also bless whatever we produce. He will bless the fruit of our body. He will bless our children. He will bless our cattle. He will bless our work. In other words, He will bless the work of our hands. He will bless our endeavors. He will give an increase to our product or our production. Keep on sowing seeds, He says, and He will give the increase. In other words, keep on working on that project, even though it seems like the boss does not care. It may seem like the boss doesn't really care. We may not get a feather in our cap. We may not get a bonus or a raise, but God says keep on working on that project and He will give the increase. We must keep on praying for the unsaved persons in our families. It may look like things are down and that they will never hearken to God's Word, but if we keep on praying for them, He will give the increase. God will bless. We must keep on witnessing to that wayward, too-hot-to-trot daughter. It may seem like there isn't any hope, but God will bless. We must keep on pray-ing in faith for that prodigal son that has dropped out of school. God will give the increase. We

God will also bless whatever we produce.

must keep on praying for that spouse that is strung out on drugs. God has promised us in a promissory con-tract that He will bless us. But we had better be careful and read the fine print.

God Will Bless Our Travel

God says in verse 5, He will bless our basket in the store. I thought I would see what some biblical schol-ars thought about this verse. Most biblical scholars do not agree that this necessarily refers to a grocery store, and I concur with them. In biblical days people trav-eled with baskets. So really God is saying, He will bless our suitcases. He will bless our Samsonite, or nowa-days, our Gucci bags. God is saying that He will bless our traveling. I travel a lot and am so glad that God blesses my travel. I am so glad that when I step on Delta Air Lines, I have a promise-keeper who has signed a contract with me. He has promised to give me grace and mercy in my travel.

God Will Bless Our Coming and Going

Then God says, in verse 6, if we harken diligently, He will bless our coming in and our going out. In other words, when we leave home, we will know everything will be all right when we get back home. If we hearken diligently, we won't have to worry about Jody coming to our house. We know about Jody. He is the one who will get our girl and be gone. If we hearken diligently, we won't have to worry about the milkman or the mailman. When we go out, we won't have to worry about who else is coming in, and when we come in, we don't have to worry about who is going out the back door. God will bless our coming in and our going out.

God is saying that He will bless our traveling.

God Will Bless Us by Kicking the Devil's Tail

In verse 7 God says, hearken to the Lord and the Lord will smite our enemies. The enemy will come in one way and go out seven ways. Do we hear what the Lord is saying? First of all, He is going to take care of our enemies. They will be smitten. Our enemies will come in over here (one way), and when God gets through with them, they will go out over there, there, there, there, there, there, and there (seven ways). Our enemies will come in one door, and God will run them out seven different doors. God will bless us by continually kicking the devil's tail.

Reading the Fine Print

God has blessed us. He is a promise-keeper, and He has given us a contract. But we need to read the fine print. There is some fine print in every contract. Usually it is preceded by some little subjunctive clause or something that says "if." When we read a contract, we should read it and look for "buts" and "ifs." God also

God will bless us by continually kicking the devil's tail.

has some "ifs," so we need to read the fine print. One of the things that bothers me about this passage, and other passages, is that they come very close to falling into the category of what has been labeled *prosperity gospel*. It bothers me when I hear folks on TV talking about "name it and claim it," believing that we can speak something into existence. No! No! No! The blessings in this passage come awfully close to that, but we need to read the fine print. There is such a thing as "self-talk." Self-talk is a motivational technique, but it is not a biblical principle. When I was younger and was still playing tennis, I used it. I talked to myself. When I was behind, I would say, "Come on McCalep." When I tossed the ball up, I would say, "Get it up higher McCalep, get it up higher." When I hit my backhand, I would say, "Keep your elbows straight McCalep." I was talking to myself. "McCalep you can do it. You've got to win this one." I was talking to myself and it was helping me to win the game. If we are salesmen working in corporate America, we will be taught to self-talk. It is a technique used in physical fitness. I talk to myself. "I've got to go and get on my Total Gym and I've got to ride my treadmill. Come on McCalep, five more minutes." I am talking to myself because it helps me exercise. If I am dieting, I have to talk to myself. I can't eat everything that everybody else eats. "McCalep, you've got to put that lemon pie back." I can use an audiotape if I wish. I can play that tape every morning when I get up: "Don't eat lemon

When we read a contract, we should read it and look for "buts" and "ifs." God also has some "ifs" so we need to read the fine print.

pie. Don't eat that lemon pie." And I will stop eating lemon pie. Although I use self-talk as a motivational technique, I do not regard it as, or claim it to be, a biblical principle. Self-talk claimed as a biblical principle steals God's glory. It slaps God in the face, and it denies that He is the blesser.

Reading the fine print, I see some of those little "ifs" in here. In verse 2 you find, "And all these blessings shall come on thee and overtake thee, *if . . .*" In verse 9, "the LORD shall establish thee an holy people unto himself, as he hath sworn unto thee, *if . . .*" Our problem is that we are not reading the fine print. We want the blessing, but we don't want to obey the fine print.

God has signed a contract with us. He is a promise-keeper. We need to get away from this prosperity gospel that puts us under the false illusion that we have the power to speak a blessing into existence. What about the people suffering through floods and other natural tragedies? Do we think that God has forsaken them for some reason or another? We need to understand that God is God, and God is God all by Himself, and God will always be God.

> *Self-talk claimed as a biblical principle steals God's glory.*

If we hearken unto Him, we will never be the tail. In verse 12, the scripture says that we won't be the borrowers, we will be the lenders. Hear what God is saying. He says, we won't be the receivers, we will be the givers. Indeed, it is better to give than to receive. I can't understand why people pray only to receive stuff. I don't want to just receive, but I want to just give. I don't think we have thought this through. We should want to be the givers also. But we pray to receive—let me receive this and that, and some money. I am praying to give some money. We need to check ourselves out. It is more blessed to give than to receive.

Needs vs. Wants

The Bible says that God will supply all of our needs according to His riches in glory (Philippians 4:19). He is a good supplier. He will supply our needs, not our wants. As a matter of fact, the Bible tells us that the Lord is our Shepherd, we shall not want. The reason why we have not been blessed is that we have been dealing too much

We need to get away from this prosperity gospel that puts us under the false illusion that we have the power to speak a blessing into existence.

in the wanting business and too little with our need business. God says He will supply all of our needs according to His riches in glory. Do we know that our

Father is rich? Do we know that we are joint heirs to the throne with Jesus? Do we know that everything that Jesus owns, we own? Do we know that Jesus is not just our Savior, but He is our elder brother? Do we know that our Father owns all the cattle on the hills? Do we know that the earth is His and the fullness thereof? And He says He will supply *ALL* of our needs.

Blessings that Follow Us

I like what verses 1 and 2 say . . . if you hearken diligently, blessings will overtake you. In another chapter, I talk about blessings following us. In other words, wherever we go, surely goodness and mercy will follow us all the days of our life. When we got saved, goodness and mercy started following us. Isn't that a good thing to know? When we go into our prayer closets, never to come out again, and take that

The reason why we have not been blessed is that we have been dealing too much in the wanting business and too little with our need business.

heavenly journey . . . when we drop this robe of flesh and take that flight, guess what . . . goodness and mercy will follow us. When we stand before the throne of God, goodness and mercy will be there pleading our case.

Blessings God Puts in Front of Us

God has some other blessings. Goodness and mercy have our backs, but God has blessings that will overtake us. Do we know what that means? It means that there are going to be some blessings that will run ahead of us. So not only do we have blessings behind us, but some blessings are going to run in front of us. This means that everywhere we go we will be bumping into blessings. When we turn this way, we bump into blessings. When we go another way, we bump into some more blessings. When we go yet another way, we bump into some grace. When we go over here, we bump into some goodness. When we go over there, we bump into some love. Mercy back there, grace up here . . . God is a promise-keeper, if we hearken diligently. If we hearken diligently, He will bless us.

> *If you hearken diligently, blessings will overtake you.*

Summary

God has promised in His Word that if we hear His voice clearly, including reading the fine print, He will bless us in an especially powerful way. The word "hear" in the Bible means "do." So if we do what He has commanded us to do, we will be blessed. The promised blessings include 1) blessing us anywhere, 2) blessing our efforts, 3) blessing our travel, 4) blessing our coming in and going out, and 5) blessing us by smiting our enemy. We must realize that we cannot speak anything into existence because it is God who is the blesser. Self-talk is a great motivational principle, but it is not a biblical one. Self-talk claimed as a biblical principle steals God's glory because it denies that He is the blesser. There is a thin line between prosperity gospel and standing on the promises of the true, greatest and only promise-keeper. Again, we are cautioned to read the fine print in the promise-keeper's contract list of promises. Usually the fine print is proceeded by a little subjunctive clause that begins with "if." God has promised that if we hearken to (do) His will, He will make us the head and not the tail, and everywhere we go blessings will overtake us. In other words, if we hearken diligently to His voice, we will be so blessed that we will bump into blessings as we journey through life.

Not only do we have blessings behind us, but some blessings are going to run in front of us. This means that everywhere we go we will be bumping into blessings.

CHAPTER TWO

Blessed Through Faith

Genesis 12:1–3 (KJV)

1 Now the LORD had said unto Abram, Get thee out of thy country, and from thy kindred, and from thy father's house, unto a land that I will shew thee:

2 And I will make of thee a great nation, and I will bless thee, and make thy name great; and thou shalt be a blessing:

3 And I will bless them that bless thee, and curse him that curseth thee: and in thee shall all families of the earth be blessed.

33

Romans 4:13 (KJV)

13 *For the promise, that he should be the heir of the world, was not to Abraham, or to his seed, through the law, but through the righteousness of faith.*

We all want to be blessed. Here is good news for us today: we can be blessed. I can guarantee it because I know the key that unlocks the door to blessing. The key is faith. Faith is the key that unlocks the door of blessing.

Two simple propositions undergird God's promise of blessing. One is that God promises blessings to those who have faith. Second, it is impossible to please God without faith. Therefore, faith lets us please God and be blessed. Faith is a deal too good to refus. Faith pleases God and faith blesses us. Notice there is a promise that if we please God, He will bless us. Faith is the key that unlocks the blessing door.

> God promises blessings to those who have faith.

A Biblical Example

Our Old Testament text from Genesis, the first book of the Bible, is a very pivotal point in all

Christianity; it is where God called out Abraham to look for a city.

The blessings that are available to us today began with the promises God made to Abraham, the father of faith. Look at Abraham. God called Abraham to go and look for a city—to go to a foreign country. He was called to go, not knowing where he was going. He was called to go, not knowing whom he would meet when he reached his destination.

> *The blessings that are available to us today began with the promises God made to Abraham, the father of faith.*

He was called to go, not knowing where he would eat or where he would sleep or where he would live. He was just called to go. Sometimes God asks you just to step out on faith. God says go, so all you need to do is just go.

Abraham's experience illustrates the biblical definition of faith. The writer of Hebrews says, "*Now faith is the substance of things hoped for, the evidence of things not seen*" (Heb. 11:1 - KJV). In other words, something that is evident yet we have not seen it. If we can see something, we can't call it faith. If we can reason it, we can't call it faith. If we can put it into a framework of deductive reasoning or inductive reasoning and have a rational predictable outcome, then we cannot call it faith.

Church Application

In the twenty-two years of my pastorate, we have never set a budget without including a faith factor. We have never done a budget without setting it beyond what we could see. Some would set the budget based on last year's income. That's the way a good account-ant would do it. They would ask, "What came in last year?" The accountant would then set the budget and project how to spend the money based upon last year's income. To set a budget that way is saying you don't expect God to do anything differently. It is a slap in God's face to set a budget like corporations set budgets. God says we walk not by sight but by faith. We have to get out on a limb if we're going to have some faith and let God do it. Last year we set a budget for $500,000 more than the year before. Guess what? We made it. Who did it? God did it because we stepped out on faith.

If we can see something, we can't call it faith.

Individual Application

In our personal lives we have to step out on faith. Too many of us are holding on to the trunk of the tree. Faith is out on the limb. We have to turn loose of the trunk and go out on that limb. Faith is the evidence of things unseen. The question that we have to raise is, "How do we have evidence of what we cannot see?" We have to raise that question to God and in light of Scripture. The Bible tells us that faith is not as blind as we often think. Faith is blind, yet faith can see. How? Faith is the evidence of things unseen, which means faith is blind, yet faith can see. The answer is that God never asked us just to have faith. God asked us to have faith in Him.

The Promises Undergirded

Faith in God undergirds the promises of God. Having faith in God underwrites the promises of God. What does it mean when something is underwritten? An example would be our church wanting to build a bigger sanctuary. We might have a bond issue for building, but some companies would underwrite the bond.

God never asked us just to have faith. God asked us to have faith in Him.

When a company underwrites a bond, it means that company guarantees they will pay the bond issue. Faith underwrites the promises of God. Faith guarantees that His promises will be paid. God uses faith to underwrite His promises.

God's Promise to Abraham and Us

Look what God promised Abraham in our Scripture text. First, He promised Abraham that He would make him a great nation. God told Abraham when he started out, not knowing where he was going, He would bless him and make his name great. Second, God promised to make Abraham a blessing. In other words God is saying, "Not only will you be blessed, but I'm going to make you a blessing." Then He promised, "I will bless the ones that bless you, and I will curse the ones that curse you."

Faith underwrites the promises of God. Faith guarantees that His promises will be paid.

God says to Abraham, "I will bless all your seed." Isn't that wonderful that He said He would bless all of Abraham's seed? Abraham is the father of faith. We are all of the seed of Abraham. All these blessings that Scripture mentions are available to Abraham's seed. That means us. Romans 4:16 (KJV) says, *"Therefore, it is of faith, that it might be by grace; to the end the promises might be sure to all the seed; not to that only which is of the law, but to that also which is of the faith of Abraham; who is the father of us all."*

God says that I can be in the blessing channel. By faith, God has promised to make us a blessing. By faith, God has promised to bless us. By faith, God has promised to bless others who bless us and to curse others who curse us. Somebody asked, "Why haven't you been mad in twenty years of pastoring?" I don't have to fight anybody. My wife used to ask me when I first started pastoring why I didn't fight back? I don't have to fight back. I never fight. I'm through fighting. My fighting days left when I left the world and got in the blessing channel. All I have to do is bless God and He will bless me. By faith. God said, "I will bless the church, the nation in which you pastor." God is blessing me right now. But God promised blessings to all of us, not just to me, but to all of Abraham's seed.

Abraham is the father of faith. We are all of the seed of Abraham. All these blessings that Scripture mentions are available to Abraham's seed.

What then is our problem? Our problem is that we are too stressed to be blessed. Conversely, Dr. Suzan Johnson-Cook titled her book *Too Blessed to Be Stressed.* Our problem is just the opposite. We are too stressed to be blessed. We are too stressed out on loving the blessing and not loving the One who blesses. We love what God can bless us with, but we aren't loving God. We are too stressed out on self to be blessed by God. God will not bless a lover of self and things. Our problem is that we have our eyes on the blessing, and we need to have our eyes on the Blesser. God will not bless a lover of houses and of cars. God will not bless a lover of clothes and of money. God blesses those who bless Him. We have our eyes on blessings when we should have our eyes on the Blesser.

Personal Testimony

In 1973, I was listed in *Business Enterprise* as an up and coming millionaire, trying to get a seat on the New York Stock Exchange. I had six financial securities licenses in seven different states. I am so thankful that God didn't let me go through with that plan. I'm glad He didn't allow me to be a millionaire. Why? Because if I had, I wouldn't be here today. I would be dead. I wasn't handling my good fortune well at that time. Some of us can't handle the blessings that we ask of God. You have to be ready to be blessed.

We are too stressed to be blessed.

Someone blessed me with an expensive suit. If somebody spilled coffee on my expensive suit, no problem. God blessed me with it in the first place, and

He will bless me with another one. Where did the suit come from? Where did the silk tie come from? Where did the dress come from? If God blessed you once, don't you think He will bless you again? What makes you think He's out of the blessing business? You have to be in the flow of blessings to be blessed.

Faith and Blessings

I want to share with you three things concerning faith that ties into blessings. First, faith blesses us with righteousness: *"Now the Lord had said unto Abram, Get thee out of thy country, and from thy kindred, and from thy father's house, unto a*

We should have our eyes on the Blesser.

land that I will shew thee" (Genesis 12:1 - KJV). Romans 4:13 (KJV) says, *"For the promise, that he should be the heir to the world, was not to Abraham, or to his seed, through the law, but through the righteous-ness of faith."*

We should be concerned with the righteousness of faith. God takes our faith and makes our wrongs right. That's what the Bible says. How else can we be righteous? All of us are wrong. If we think we're right, we're wrong. We may have been reading psychology books that say, "I'm okay, you're okay." We're not okay. Read the Bible. All have sinned and fallen short of the glory of God. All of us. Can we find a righteous man? No, not one. Romans 4:25 (KJV) says, *"Who was delivered for our offences, and was raised again for our justification."* By the resurrection of Jesus, we are justified.

What does it mean to be justified? It means to be made right. That's why the song says, "In His righteousness I stand complete." God takes our faith and turns our incompleteness into something complete. God takes our faith and turns our wrong into right. God takes our unholiness and changes it into holiness. God takes our imperfections and turns them into perfections. How else do we dare stand in a sanctuary in the presence of God and say we are raising holy hands? We dare to do so because God takes our faith and makes unholy hands holy. God, by faith, justifies us.

Faith blesses us with righteousness.

It's a blessing to be justified. Faith blesses us with justification and righteousness. Faith blesses us with perfection and holiness. God can take our little faith, even if it's as weak and little as a mustard seed, and turn it into righteousness in His name.

Second, faith blesses us with grace. Romans 4:16 (KJV) says, *"Therefore it is of faith, that it might be by grace."* Do we need some grace? If so, we'd better have some faith. Although grace is an undeserved, unmerited, free gift of God, faith invokes grace. We all need grace. *"For by grace are ye saved through faith"* (Ephesians 2:8 - KJV). Faith ignites grace and sets grace on fire. Faith sends grace running to a lost sinner. Faith sends grace running in our time of need, in our adversity, in our trials and tribulations, in our wickedness, in our evilness, in our wrongness. Faith sends grace to us to hug us and love us when we aren't loveable.

Finally, a third thing about faith is that it guarantees the promises of God: *"Therefore it is of faith, that it might be by grace; to the end the promise might be sure"* (Romans 4:16 - KJV).

> Faith blesses us with grace.

Faith undergirds the promises. Faith guarantees the promises of God. I don't know about you, but I'm standing on the promises. Are you standing on the promises? The songwriter said, "I'm standing on the promises of Christ my King, through eternal ages let His praises ring." If you're standing on the promises, you'd better have faith. If you're standing on the promises with no faith, you're standing on shifting, sinking sand. We must have faith. We are indeed blessed through faith.

If we want to be blessed, keep the faith and give God glory. Romans 4:20 (KJV) says, *"He staggered not at the promise of God through unbelief; but was strong in faith, giving glory to God."* Abraham was strong in the faith, giving glory to God. Abraham kept the faith and gave glory to God. If we want to be blessed, keep the faith and give glory to God. We are indeed blessed through faith.

Summary

Faith is the key that unlocks the door of blessings. Faith lets us please God and be blessed. Faith pleases God and faith blesses us. The promise is that if we please God, He will bless us.

Faith in God undergirds the promises of God. God never asks us just to have faith; rather, God asks that we have faith in Him. Having faith in God underwrites (guarantees) the promises of God.

Faith guarantees the promises of God.

God promised Abraham, the father of faith, multiple blessings, including the promise that "I will bless your seed." We are all of the seed of Abraham. Therefore, all the blessings that were promised to Abraham are available to us. There is a definite relationship between faith and blessings. Three things concerning faith that relate to blessings are 1) faith blesses us with righteousness, 2) faith blesses us with grace, and 3) faith guarantees the promises of God.

CHAPTER THREE

Blessed Through Blessing

Genesis 12:1–3 (KJV)

1 *Now the LORD had said unto Abram, Get thee out of thy country, and from thy kindred, and from thy father's house, unto a land that I will shew thee:*

2 *And I will make of thee a great nation, and I will bless thee, and make thy name great; and thou shalt be a blessing:*

3 *And I will bless them that bless thee, and curse him that curseth thee: and in thee shall all families of the earth be blessed.*

Let's review the seven blessings that God promised to Abraham that are available to us. We find them in

Genesis 12:1–3. God said to Abraham, "I will make you a great nation; I will bless you and make your name great; I will make you a blessing; I will bless them that bless you; I will curse them that curse you, and all your family shall be blessed."

What a wonderful promise God has made available to us that He will bless our name. He will bless our seed, our entire family. He will make us a blessing. He will even bless those that bless us. And He has promised that He will curse those that come up against us. This promise is given and it's assured that we have the availability of all these promises.

If we bless God and bless others, we will be blessed.

The question then arises, how do we get these blessings? How do we find favor in God?

Bless God and Others and Be Blessed

I propose that if we bless God and bless others, we will be blessed. Most of us know that when praises go up, blessings come down. One way that we bless God is with praises. When we send blessings up, blessings come down. When we bless God, God blesses us.

Also, when blessings go out, blessings come in. We serve not only a vertical cross that reaches up to God, but we also serve a horizontal cross that reaches out to man. Some just want to serve a one-way cross, but it's a two-way cross. We have to bless God and we have to bless others. We can't do 50 percent.

When blessings go up, blessings come down. When blessings go out, blessings come in. These are spiritual laws of God. It's just as sure as God's physical laws. "What goes up must come down" is called Newton's Law of Gravity, but Newton only discovered it. It is God's physical law. And as sure as what goes up must come down, when blessings go up, blessings come down; when blessings go out, blessings come in.

Some have a difficult time with blessing others. If we want to be blessed, we need to have a mind set of blessing others. The Bible says, *"And be not conformed to this world: but be ye transformed by the renewing of your mind, that ye may prove what is that good, and acceptable, and perfect, will of God"* (Romans 12:2 - KJV). We need to begin right now trying to renew our

> When blessings go up, blessings come down. When blessings go out, blessings come in.

minds that we may bless others. When we get up in the morning, we should look for an opportunity to bless somebody. Often I make sure I have some money in my pocket so if I meet somebody who needs some money, I can bless them. I didn't put the money in my pocket for me. I leave home looking for an opportunity. I know that I want to bless somebody everyday in some way.

The psalmist said, *"Bless the Lord, O my soul: and all that is within me, bless his holy name"* (Psalm 103:1-KJV). So when blessings go up, blessings come down. When blessings go out, blessings come in. We need to understand that God wants to bless us. It is His perfect will that we abide in His blessing channel. God wants to bless you. God wants to bless all of us.

Backslidden From Being Blessed

So the question still remains, "Why aren't more of us blessed?" The problem is that we have backslidden out of the blessing channel of God. We've gotten out of the rivers of blessing. It's like driving a car on the highway and slipping over into a ditch. If it's a deep ditch, we stay there until we can get back on the highway. Many are driving in the ditch rather than driving on the highway of blessings. Many of us have lost our blessings. Our blessings have been rejected. We are like Esau. He sold his birthright and got tricked out of his blessing (Genesis 25:30–34).

We have backslidden out of the blessing channels of God.

Lost Blessings

Esau was Jacob's twin brother, a son of Isaac and Rebekah, and a grandson of Abraham. Esau was the older twin. Esau is the one we should sing about, when we sing, "We are climbing Jacob's ladder." But instead we sing about Jacob because Esau sold his blessing.

Esau was tricked. He sold his birthright. He was busy with the business of life and didn't take time to find out what was happening around him or what God was already doing with him. Esau was so busy hunting and doing other things. He was so tired, impatient and impetuous that he sold his birthright for a bowl of pottage.

Many today are contemporary Esaus. We are so busy doing life that we are missing life. We are so busy hunting for material stuff that the evil one has entered in and we are unaware like Esau. God wants to bless us, but we are denying our blessings. Our blessings have been taken away from us. We are so busy with self—all our accomplishments, who we are, and what we are trying to be—that Satan has pulled us off the blessing highway. Now we are driving in the ditch. We are in the gutter. We are out of the blessing channel and need deliverance.

Deliverance Needed

If we want to be blessed, we need to be delivered from two things. First, we need to be delivered from materialism. We need to be delivered from our love of things. Too many of us are still praying for things, external things. Solomon was one of the richest men in the Bible. He didn't ask God to be rich. He asked God for wisdom, and the wisdom of God made him rich. We need to be delivered from materialism. Second, we need deliverance from self. Our "self" won't let us be blessed.

> We are so busy with self—all our accomplishments, who we are, and what we are trying to be—that Satan has pulled us off the blessing highway.

Personal Testimony

I used to be a victim of materialism. I loved stuff and wanted to be a millionaire by the age of twenty-seven. This was my goal; I had it written down. In 1973 I bought two new cars. I bought a 1973 Cadillac Brougham with the fancy roof. I thought I was somebody. I would drive it into my yard in Shaker Heights, Ohio, put my little tape on, and listen to Lou Rawls talking about I'm glad I have a piece of the pie. God had to deliver me from materialism.

All I asked God for when I moved to Atlanta, Georgia was peace and happiness. That is all I asked from God after He delivered me from materialism. All I wanted was peace. My wife and family knew this. When they asked me what I wanted for my birthday or for Christmas, I wanted peace and happiness.

Although God has blessed me to be a pastor, I never asked to be pastor of a 6,000-member megachurch as I am today. I didn't see a vision of such a situation. In fact, I like small churches. It would have been all right with me if our membership never increased to more than 100 members. We could have stopped at 200 and I would have been happy. I care, but it doesn't matter whether our membership is 100 or 10,000. I do care that 100 percent of whatever we are doing is fulfilling the purposes of God.

We need to understand that there is a blessing on the other side of materialism. If we can get delivered from materialism, there's a blessing on the other side. God has promised that if we're faithful over a few things, He will make us rulers over many things. We need to be faithful over a few and God will give us much.

If we want to be blessed, we not only have to *be* delivered from materialism, we have to *stay* delivered from materialism. We may say, "I'm already blessed."

God has a word for us today. He says we had better get delivered quickly because we'll lose that blessing. Just because we have something, a nice car and a nice house, it doesn't have to be there forever. We'd better seek deliverance.

Just because we're driving around believing we have a piece of the pie, doesn't mean we can't lose our material blessings quickly. In 1973 I was netting $73,000 a year. In 1973 that was surely a whole lot. When I moved to Georgia, the Dean at Georgia State offered me a job. The job paid $14,000 a year.

God cut me down from $73,000 to $14,000. He took a house in Shaker Heights away from me that today would be valued at over half a million dollars, and put me in an apartment complex in Clarkston, Georgia with my wife, three boys, and a dog. He took me from those two cars I had, to no car. I rode MARTA buses; the same MARTA on whose board of directors I'm currently serving. I didn't have tokens to ride that bus. Not so long ago, as a member of the board of directors of MARTA, I helped make a decision on a $243 million proposal.

I didn't have a car when I came to Georgia. In 1976 I walked to the A&P supermarket and pushed my

> If we want to be blessed, we not only have to be delivered from materialism, we have to stay delivered from materialism.

basket approximately three miles back to my apartment. I have a word of caution to those who drive big cars and live in big houses: If you haven't been delivered from materialism, you better get delivered quickly. God can snatch things from under you just as fast as He gave it to you.

Deliverance from Self

Second, as mentioned, if we want to be blessed, we need to also be delivered from ourselves. Our "self" won't let us be blessed. God is trying to bless us but "self" won't get out of the way. Self manufactures pride, and pride is the enemy of blessings. We need to pray, "Lord, deliver us from 'self.'"

If we want to be blessed, we need to also be delivered from ourselves.

Self won't let us bless others because self is jealous. Self won't let us bless others because self is envious. Self won't even let us bless God, for self has too much pride. Every time we try to praise God, every time we try to bless God, self and pride get in the way and pride tells self to chill out.

Everything is not about you and me. We think it's all about us, but it's not about us at all. It's about God. We have to get self out of the way. That's what the writer meant when he said, "Let go and let God." Let go of self. Get out of the way. Stop blocking your blessing.

Repentance Needed

Before being delivered from materialism and self, we have to repent. This is a serious topic. If we want to be blessed, we have to repent. Change cannot come without repentance. Revival cannot come without repentance. We cannot be delivered from materialism unless we repent. We cannot be delivered from self unless we repent. We cannot be ready for a blessing until we repent. We can hear a message and receive it, but unless we repent, it's just information. We go to church and become more knowledgeable on how to find favor with God, but we will not find favor unless we repent. Nothing happens until we repent.

> Before being delivered from materialism and self, we have to repent.

Unless we repent, there is no change. Unless we repent, there is no transformation. Unless we repent, there is no revival. I often fear that Sunday after Sunday many of us hear a message, receive the message, go to Sunday School, hear God's Word, and read our Bibles during the week but fail to repent. Change cannot occur without repentance.

In Matthew 3:2 (KJV), John the Baptist is saying, *"Repent ye: for the kingdom of heaven is at hand."* He is saying to repent because there's a blessing waiting for us and it's right around the corner. Repent because there's a blessing standing at our doorstep. The blessing wants to come in, but we have to be delivered and we can't be delivered unless we repent.

Sometime ago, God showed me I was not leading His people in praise and worship as He called us and created us to do. I fell on my knees and repented for that wrong. Several years ago, God told me we were not doing enough in discipleship. I was too busy making Christians and not making disciples. Once again I repented.

You need to repent and be blessed. You may be the same as I was in 1973, you may have a love for material stuff; if so, you need to bow your head and repent and be blessed. You may know that self is in the way. You need to repent and be delivered so you can bless others—your neighbor, your pastor. You need to repent so you can bless your brother, your sister, and your coworker. You need to repent and be delivered so you can even bless your enemy because the Bible clearly says to bless those that despise you and come up against you and curse you. You ought to bless even them.

Unless we repent, nothing really happens. We need to repent from self so we can bless the Lord. We ought to bless Him with our service, stewardship, talents, gifts, love, money, worship and our praise. But we have to repent and be delivered so we can bless Him.

God Is Able

Finally, as stated in the previous chapter, we have to have faith that He, who is the Blesser, is able to perform. Abraham staggered not at the promises of God through unbelief. Standing on the promises is quite different from staggering on the promises. Some of us are staggering. A drunk man staggers. A drunk man can hardly hold up his head or walk straight. Abram did not stagger on the promises, but he stood on the promises and gave glory to God.

We need to know that He who did the promising is able to fulfill them. God is able. God is able to take a little boy's lunch and feed 5,000. He is able to deliver Daniel from the lion's den. He is able to lead three Hebrew boys through a fiery furnace. Why didn't that fire burn them? Because He is able.

I've been through the flooding rivers, but it did not overcome me. I've been through the fire, but it did not consume me. Why? Because He is able. He who has given the promise is able to perform. He has promised that if I bless Him and others, I will continually be blessed. We are blessed through blessing.

Summary

In Genesis 12:1–3, God promises Abram, and us, the seed of Abram, a sevenfold blessing. First, I will make you a great nation. Second, I will bless you. Third, I will make your name great. Fourth, I will make you a blessing. Fifth, I will bless them that bless you. Sixth, I will curse them that curse you. Seventh, I will bless your family. The key to receiving these blessings is to bless God and others. For indeed, when blessings go up, blessings come down. And when blessings go out, blessings come in. Many of us, however, have backslidden from our blessings and/or lost our blessings. To regain our blessings and get back into the flow of God's blessings, we must repent and be delivered from materialism and self. Further, we must continually stand on the promises of God without staggering—ever-knowing and trusting that the God who made the promises is well able to perform and fulfill them.

Standing on the promises is quite different from staggering on the promises.

Blessed Through the Power of Thinking

2 Corinthians 10:5 (KJV)

⁵ Casting down imaginations, and every high thing that exalteth itself against the knowledge of God, and bringing into captivity every thought to the obedience of Christ.

Philippians 4:8,9 (TLB)

⁸ Fix your thoughts on what is true and good and right. Think about things that are pure and lovely, and dwell on the fine, good things in others. Think about all you can praise God for and be glad about.

*⁹Keep putting into practice all you learned
from me and saw me doing, and the God of
peace will be with you.*

As we begin this chapter, I'd like to plant two seeds. Prayerfully these two seedlings will grow as we water and cultivate them and depend on God to give the increase.

First, God has given us the power to govern our thoughts. Second, obedient thoughts produce a blessed life. Think blessed and be blessed. We can be blessed through the power of thinking.

Dr. Norman Vincent Peale wrote a bestselling secular book entitled *The Power of Positive Thinking*. The book has sold well over a million copies, and it's still selling today. A similar book by Earl Nightingale is entitled *Think and Grow Rich*. Although these books probably were written for secular motives and secular reasons, they were based upon a spiritual principle: If we bring our thoughts into obedience to the mind and the will of Christ, we will be blessed. Too often Christians shy away from what is lifted up in the secular world because we think it belongs to the devil and the world. But we need to understand that God created all things good and perfect.

> *Think blessed and be blessed.*

Stinking Thinking

I want to tear down strongholds of what I call stinking thinking and enter the realm of spiritual thought modification. We need to under-stand that thoughts are powerful. Positive thoughts are powerful. Also, negative thoughts are pow-erful. For the believer, all negative thoughts relate to past failures,

> *For the Christian, negative thinking is not just negative thinking; negative thinking is embracing the dead.*

wrongs, sin, guilt, and betrayal that have not yet been crucified. The Bible tells us very clearly that we were dead in our trespasses, but God has made us alive in Christ (Romans 6:11). So, for the Christian, negative thinking is not just negative thinking; negative think-ing is embracing the dead.

"For to be carnally minded is death; but to be spiri-tually minded is life and peace" (Romans 8:6 - KJV). *"And if Christ be in you, the body is dead because of sin; but the Spirit is life because of righteousness. But if the Spirit of him that raised up Jesus from the dead dwell in you, he that raised up Christ from the dead shall also quicken your mortal bodies by his Spirit that dwelleth in you"* (Romans 8:10,11 - KJV). For the believer, negative thinking is being intimate with what is dead.

You wouldn't bring to the dinner table a loved one who has died. You wouldn't put a corpse in your car and take it to work with you. You wouldn't sleep with a dead man. The dead should be buried. The reason some of us are not more blessed is that we're eating and sleeping with our dead trespasses which should be buried.

You go to work and our thinking is stinking because you really have a corpse with you. You ought to ask yourself when you're riding to work, "Who is on the other side of the car, a corpse or a living Jesus?" The dead stinks. That's why I choose to call this stinking thinking. Our sins died; Christ crucified them. He cast them into the sea of forgetfulness never to rise again (Hebrews 10:17). But we keep searching and diving and bringing them ashore.

> *For the believer, negative thinking is being intimate with what is dead.*

Who's on the Cross and Who's on the Throne?

Who's on the cross and who's on the throne? Many of us live as if Christ is on the cross and our past thoughts, sins, and guilt are on the throne. The solution is to put your past thoughts on the cross and put Christ on the throne. We need to understand that Jesus is not on the cross. He's on the throne.

Some of us wear crucifixes around our necks. Do you know what a crucifix is? It's a cross that has Christ on the cross. How sad it would be if right now we had Jesus hanging upon that cross. Jesus is not on the cross. He lives. He's risen. We have it reversed. We're wearing Jesus on the cross,

> *Put your past thoughts on the cross and put Christ on the throne.*

we're living like Jesus is still on the cross, and we have placed our thoughts and ourselves on the throne. We need to reverse it. We need to take our burdens to the cross, nail them up there, crucify our past thoughts and put Jesus on the throne. Who's on the throne is very important.

In West Africa, the Ashanti people have an interesting primitive religion. They revere a golden stool that supposedly came down from God, and they worship the stool. The Ashanti are also slave traders who fought the British. They fought the British eight times in six wars. They won many battles against the British and not as many of them went into slavery. The British king, however, wanted that golden throne. He wanted to sit on that throne. The strong Ashanti Queen Mother, Yaa Asantewa, whose hero status is synonymous to America's Rosa Parks, took up the mantle and led her people to victory to assure that the British king would never sit on that throne. I'm thankful many Ashanti have become Christians, but if the chief becomes a Christian, he has to give up the throne (stool).

Who's on the throne in our lives? It appears that too many of us still have our pasts on the throne. And so we have guilt feelings that we must bring into obedience to the power of God. We have to take our sins, nail them to the cross, and make Jesus King on the throne.

Obedient Thinking

In 2 Corinthians 10:4 we read about pulling down strongholds. This is the only place in the New Testament that the word "strongholds" is used. We must declare spiritual warfare against negative, stinking thinking. The metaphor Paul uses in 2 Corinthians 10 is one of a soldier, a fighter. Paul talks about weapons. He says our weapons are not carnal; the weapons we use are spiritual. Paul talks about tearing down strongholds and casting down every imagination. Every imagination, every thought must be locked up. Every thought must be put away and sent to obedience boot camp. Every thought must become obedient to the power that God has given man.

> We must declare spiritual warfare against negative, stinking thinking.

After we send our dog to obedience school, if we tell him to sit, he'll sit. Sometimes we get thoughts, and we need to speak to those thoughts, "Sit." When that old thinking comes up about somebody who has betrayed us, we need to say, "Sit." When men see that fine, young lady walking down the hall at the office with that tight skirt on, they need to say, "Sit!" When ladies meet that handsome guy on the elevator who's looking good early in the morning, they need to say, "Sit!"

> We have to bring into captivity every imagination, every thought that is not of the knowledge and the mind of God.

We have to bring into captivity every imagination, every thought that is not of the knowledge and the mind of God. Stinking thinking allows our past sins to block us from the view of the presence of God. We can't see God for stinking thinking. That's why David the psalmist cried out, *"Create in me a clean heart, O God; and renew a right spirit within me"* (Psalm 51:10 - KJV). We cannot see the presence of God because we have a corpse riding with us to work. We need to kick that corpse out of our cars. We were dead in our trespasses, but we have become alive in His righteousness. We need to bury the dead and let the dead stay dead. It corrupts our minds to have this stinking thinking.

Count Your Blessings

Consider blessed thinking rather than stinking thinking. Thinking blessed means counting our blessings one by one. Paul writes about joy from a jail cell in Rome to the church at Philippi and to us. In a dungeon with little light, Paul faces impending death. Yet, Paul gives these words to us: *"Always be full of joy in the Lord; I say it again, rejoice!"* (Philippians 4:4- TLB). The King James Version says, *"Rejoice in the Lord alway: and again I say, Rejoice."*

Paul goes on to say in Philippians 4:5–8 (KJV), *"Let your moderation be known unto all men. The Lord is at hand. Be careful for nothing; but in every thing by prayer and supplication with thanksgiving let your requests be made known unto God. And the peace of God, which passeth all understanding, shall keep your hearts and minds through Christ Jesus. Finally, brethren, whatsoever things are true, whatsoever things are honest, whatsoever things are just, whatsoever things are pure, whatsoever things are lovely, whatsoever things are of good report; if there be any virtue, and if there be any praise, think on these things."*

> Thinking blessed means counting our blessings one by one.

The songwriter wrote, "Count your blessings, name them one by one, and you will now see what

God has done." We need to count our blessings. Number one, we are still alive. Number two, if we die, we have a home in heaven. Number three, we have clothes on our backs. Number four, we have food on our tables. Number five, we have shoes on our feet. Number six, we have a roof over our head. Number seven, we have eyes to see. Number eight, we have ears to hear. Number nine, we have legs to walk. Number ten, we have a mind to think. Number eleven, we have a soul to feel. Number twelve, we have a heart to love. And so many, many, many more. Our blessings are endless.

Bring all those evil, stinking thoughts under captivity. We must think blessed and be blessed. When evil comes, we must tell it to sit. We must treat it ruthlessly. We must put evil on the cross. We must put Jesus on the throne, for He lives. He lives.

Summary

We can be blessed through the power of thinking. God has given us the power to govern our thoughts, therefore, we should bring our imagination and thoughts into obedience with God. Many believers suffer from what has been labeled "stinking thinking." Stinking thinking is negative thinking, and for the believer negative thinking is embracing and being intimate with the dead.

We must think blessed and be blessed. We must get rid of that corpse. We must bury it and leave it buried because Jesus is alive. We must put our dead thinking on the cross and put Jesus on the throne because He is Lord. He has risen from the dead and He is Lord.

CHAPTER FIVE

Blessed Through Affliction

Psalm 119:71 (KJV)

*71 It is good for me that I have been afflicted;
that I might learn thy statutes.*

How can we be blessed through affliction? First, affliction can bring us closer to God. Second, affliction can be used to bring glory to God. Affliction can bring us closer to God and affliction can bring glory to God.

Affliction, which comes in various ways, can be packaged in many different ways. Affliction can be a sickness that just won't get well. Affliction can be a pain that just won't stop hurting or an addiction that seemingly just can't be overcome. Affliction can be a handicap that is permanent. Affliction can be an illness that may be terminal. Affliction can be nervousness that can't be calmed, a problem that can't be solved, or a mess that can't be cleaned. Affliction comes in many bags, packaged in many ways.

Trusting God in the Midst of Affliction

We have a problem trusting in God's Word in the time of affliction. We too often focus on the affliction rather than trusting in the Word of God. We've become preoccupied with what we are going through.

A preacher told a story of when he was having some tremendous problems in his church. An elderly woman invited him to her house for lunch. She fixed him a nice meal. He wanted to talk about his problems, but she just wanted to show him a picture of Daniel in the lion's den. She took him into her family room and showed him a huge picture of Daniel in the lion's den. She asked him what he saw in the picture. He said that he saw lions. She told him to keep

> We too often focus on the affliction rather than trusting in the Word of God.

looking. All he could see was a man and some lions. The old lady told him to keep on looking, but all he could see were the lions. Then she told him to look at Daniel and tell her what Daniel was doing.

Maybe you've seen this picture. Daniel is not looking at the lions. In the picture, Daniel has his face toward the heavens. When we're in the lion's den, the problem is that we are focusing on the lion. The Word of God says, don't focus on the lion, but, "look to the hills from whence cometh your help" (Psalm 121:1). Focus on God. If there's any affliction in our lives, we must stop focusing on our problems and look at the Word of God. God has given precepts: Delight in Thy Word. All things work together for the good of those who love the Lord and are the called according to His purpose.

The writer of Psalm 119 was going through something, but he didn't focus on the problem. Instead, he focused on the Word of God.

A Lesson from a Psalmist

In verse 50, the psalmist says, "The law is my comfort in my affliction: for thy word hath quickened me." The word "quickened" means made alive. By the time he gets to verse 65, he narrows his attention to simply being blessed in his affliction by the Word of God. He says in verse 67–68 and 71–72, "Before I was afflicted I went astray: but now have I kept thy Word. Thou art good, and doest good; teach me thy statutes . . . It is good for me that I have been afflicted; that I might learn thy statutes (thy word, thy law). The law of thy mouth is better unto me than thousands of gold and silver."

God's Word is a comfort to us in the time of affliction.

The psalmist says, "Before I was afflicted, I acted like a complete fool. Before I was afflicted, I went astray, but now I have kept Thy Word." The psalmist says, "I went astray, but now I have kept Thy Word, I'm back in Your will. I went astray, but now I'm keeping Your Word. I'm walking in the way. But as I look back over it, I can truly say it was good for me to have been afflicted that I might learn Your Word. If I hadn't been afflicted, I may not have known Your Word. Your Word is more precious to me now. I went astray and You taught me Your Word. Your Word brought me back. And to me now Your Word is more precious than anything on earth. There is nothing more valuable to me than Your Word."

Blessed with Comfort in Affliction

God's Word is a comfort to us in the time of affliction. "This is my comfort in my affliction: for thy word hath quickened me" (Verse 50). Even in the affliction of the hurt of a loved one's death, God's Word brings us comfort. What if we had to go to funerals with no word from God? What if the preacher doing the eulogy could not say those comforting words that we hear?

God uses affliction to correct us and humble us.

First Thessalonians 4:18 is often read at homegoing celebrations: " . . . Comfort one another with these words." In other words, these are words of comfort. Suppose we did not have these words? We are indeed blessed through affliction by His Word.

Blessed with Correction in Affliction

God uses affliction to correct us and humble us. There are some lessons that can only be learned in adversity. There are some lessons that can only be learned in the dark shadows of life. The songwriter said it well when he said if I had not had problems, how would I have ever known that God can solve them? The psalmist said, "Before I was afflicted I went astray."

God sometimes has to punish us or chastise us to make us do right. Like any loving parent, God often has to discipline us, punish us and sometimes slap us on the hand. Sometimes He has to take a switch to our legs. And at other times we are so hardheaded, He has to hit us in the head with a two-by-four. All God's punishment and chastisement are done in love, therefore, God could never be locked up for abusing one of His children.

An Opportunity to Bless God

Affliction can be used to bring glory to God. In John 9, Jesus meets a blind man and his parents. The religious folks asked Jesus, "Why is this man blind?" More specifically, they said, "Who sinned? Did his parents sin or did he sin? Why is he blind?" Jesus said, "Neither. He's blind to bring glory, to bring the manifestations of the power of God where everybody can see the good works that God has."

All God's punishment and chastisement are done in love, therefore, God could never be locked up for abusing one of His children.

If we've ever had a handicapped child, we ought to delight in this word. If we've ever had an afflicted child, we should find comfort that neither Mama, Daddy, nor the child sinned, but it can bring glory to God. If we've ever had an afflicted relative, we should understand that this can bring glory to God. If we are a product of an incestuous relationship, a bastard child, or whatever our situation may be, we should remember that the Word of God says affliction can bring Him glory.

Paul said, "I'm not going to brag about my revelations, but I'm going to brag about my infirmities. I'm going to brag about the thorn in my flesh, my affliction, because it brings glory to God. So the power of Christ can rest on me."

A Personal Testimony

I, like Paul, have a thorn in the flesh. God used my thorn to keep me from going astray; when I went astray, God put the thorn in my flesh to bring me back to where I should be. God still uses my thorn to keep me from thinking too much of myself. My body and mind were once afflicted with alcohol addiction that would not go away. An addiction that caused me much pain and much affliction. An addiction that I could not solve by myself. Jesus lifted my affliction and now I can truly say, like the psalmist, it was good that I was afflicted.

Affliction can be used to bring glory to God.

Before I was afflicted, I had gone astray, but my affliction taught me to trust in God. My affliction brought me on the right track. Even now, when I begin to think too much of myself, God just kind of twists my thorn and lets me know I'm not The Right Reverend Doctor McCalep. I'm just a nobody trying to tell everybody about somebody who will bless anybody.

Summary

We can be blessed through our affliction because affliction brings us closer to God, and God can be glorified through our afflictions. The psalmist in the 119 Psalm and the apostle Paul, speaking to the church at Corinth, teaches us powerful lessons about being blessed through affliction. The psalmist proclaims that he had gone astray, but his affliction corrected him. Therefore it was good that he was afflicted. The apostle Paul proclaims that his affliction of "a thorn in the flesh" provided a great opportunity to glorify God. We learn that through affliction we grow closer to God because God comforts us in our afflictions, and we are disciplined and corrected by our afflictions. Through it all, we are blessed through afflictions because our afflictions provide an excellent opportunity for us to bless God.

CHAPTER SIX

Blessed Through Paying the Price

Genesis 4:7,8 (KJV)

7 *If thou doest well, shalt thou not be accepted? and if thou doest not well, sin lieth at the door. And unto thee shall be his desire, and thou shalt rule over him.*

8 *And Cain talked with Abel his brother: and it came to pass, when they were in the field, that Cain rose up against Abel his brother, and slew him.*

Luke 14:28 (KJV)

28 *For which of you, intending to build a tower, sitteth not down first, and counteth the cost, whether he have sufficient to finish it?*

In a previous chapter I proposed that every blessing has a price tag. Many of us want to be blessed, but we don't want to pay the price. Some of us are in love with the image of being blessed, but when we count the cost, often decide to reject the blessings. Many of us are in love with the thought of being blessed or successful. We see others blessed and successful, and we are in love with the image and thought of being blessed as well. But, when we count the cost of being blessed, we find that we are not willing because it costs too much.

That is why some of us procrastinate and sit around trying to determine how we can be blessed without paying the cost. We claim to want to be disciples of Christ, but we don't want to pay the cost of discipleship. Salvation is free, but discipleship costs. Jesus paid it all for salvation, but we have to pay for the cost of discipleship.

Dues Required for Blessing

If we want to be truly blessed, we have to pay dues. These dues are the dues of isolation. It is lonely at the top. Also, there are the dues of rejection, criticism, envy and jealousy. If we are blessed, people will be envious and become jealous of our blessings.

Cain's Children

If we are blessed, we have to pay the price tag for the ridicule and hurt that Cain's children will put on us. If we are blessed, the children of Cain are going to hurt us. If we are blessed, the children of Cain are going to talk about us and isolate us. There is a spirit of Cain in the children of Cain that still exists in the world and in the church today.

Do we remember Cain of the two brothers Cain and Abel? God blessed Abel's sacrifice. Abel had a more acceptable sacrifice, and Cain didn't like that. So Cain rose up against his brother and slew him. The spirit of Cain still exists, and Cain's children really believe that the blessings we have belong to them.

Cain thought that Abel's blessing belonged to him, and the Cains of today really think that the blessings we have belong to them. They think that house we have really ought to be their house. They think that husbands we have really ought to be their husbands and the wives we have really ought to be their wives.

Cain's children do not want to pay the price of being blessed. They're set on pulling us back with them. So what do they do? They isolate us. They stop talking to us. We're not accepted. They want us to be a part of the unblessed group as they are. So Cain's children will criticize us. Cain's children will be jealous of us and ridicule us. They will talk about us and criticize us so we will weaken under the pressure. Then, rather than find favor with God, we want to find favor with the children of Cain.

They work on us so hard until we decide that we'd rather find favor with the children of Cain than find favor with God. If we get a big raise or a promotion on our job, some of Cain's children show up. If we are happy and positive all the time, some of Cain's children show up. Cain's children don't like positive, happy people. They will say, "What's wrong with them? They're just pretending. They aren't all that happy." If we get married to a blessed person, some of Cain's children show up. If we stay single for a while and then get married, some of Cain's children show up.

Here is a word for any single person: You need to understand that when you get married, if and when God decides to bless you in that way, you will lose some of your friends. You need to understand this fact because Cain's children will be there. They're so close to you, it's hard to discern. You must pray for the gift and power of discernment.

It's just like Judas and John sitting at the Lord's Supper. In other words, Cain's children may be sitting right beside you, all around you, close enough to give you a kiss of betrayal.

CIDS (Cain Immunity Deficiency Syndrome)

To be blessed, we have to develop immunity to Cain's children. The reason some of us can't be blessed is that we have an immunity deficiency syndrome. It's not AIDS, it's CIDS—Cain Immunity Deficiency Syndrome. It's AIDS spelled with a C. We have a deficiency syndrome. In other words, our immunity's not strong enough to fight off Cain. We're deficient in our immunity to Cain's children. The children of Cain, Granddaddy Cain, Grandmama Cain, Auntie and Uncle Cain attack us. They're all around us; our bodies and our spirits can't fight off Cain. So, Cain kills our blessings and our blessings die under the spirit of Cain. There is a solution against CIDS. There is a vaccine against Cain Immunity Deficiency Syndrome. The following will protect us from CIDS.

Blessings Come with Responsibilities

Blessings come with responsibilities. If God blesses us with a car, we have to buy gas. If we're never blessed with a car, we'd never have to buy gas. If God blesses

us with a car, that means we might have to give somebody a ride. We may be driving a car, but it's not the
car of our desire. But if God gives us the car of our
desire, we would not give anybody a ride. We would
not even let our wife drive that car. We would not let
our children drive that car and would not allow anyone to eat in it. That is why we can't be blessed with
the car of our desire.

If we're blessed with children, we have to care for
those children. God has blessed my wife and me with
three boys. We love them. I'm excited about them. I
enjoyed raising them, but guess what? I don't want
any more children. I'm blessed, but I don't want any
more. Why don't I want any more children? Because I
don't want the responsibility. I will take a few grand-
children. But even as a grandparent there is responsibility. Maybe a different responsibility, but every
blessing has a price tag on it.

Blessings come with responsibility. If men want to
be blessed with wives then they have the responsibility of loving, caring, providing, nurturing, and doing
all that God tells husbands to do. If women want to
be blessed with husbands then they have all the
responsibilities of wives. I know many widows who
say they don't want another husband. They loved the
one they had and that one went on to glory, but they

don't want another one. Why? Because they don't want the responsibility. Blessings come with responsibility.

A man at a party made an advance to another man's wife. Her husband noticed this man was coming onto his wife, winking and walking by. Finally the husband went into another room and started writing some notes. People didn't know whether he was getting a gun, or a bat, or whatever. When he returned, he approached the man and said, "Now let me show you: this is the mortgage note, here is the children's tuition, these are the dental bills, here are the two car notes. I will send you the rest of the bills the first of the month. Now if you want her, you got her." That ended his forwardness to her. Blessings come with responsibilities.

Small-Mindedness Blocks Blessings

We can't be blessed and be small-minded. We don't serve a small-minded God. We serve an extravagant Father and a big God. We serve a big-time God. So we shouldn't expect God to bless us in small-time ways. We have to increase our spiritual capacity to be blessed big-time. We have to exercise and practice the spiritual part of our lives so our spiritual parts will get bigger. We need a bigger spiritual self to hold God's big blessings. Some of our buckets are too small; our pans are too little to contain the big blessings.

A man's wife always cut off the tip of the roast and threw it away before cooking the roast. Her husband asked, "Why do you throw the tip away?" She said because her mama threw it away. He asked why did her mama throw it away. His wife said her mama threw away the tip of the roast because Grandmama threw it away. He said, "Why did Grandmama throw it away?" She said because Great-Grandmama always cut it off and threw the tip away. They always cut the tip and threw it away. Finally, they traced their roots to the Great-Great-Grandmama and found out that she always threw away the tip of the roast because her pan was too small for the whole roast.

Just like the women in this story, some of us are throwing our blessings away. Our pan is too small so we keep throwing away the tip—we're throwing our blessings away. All because of our small-mindedness. We have to increase our spiritual capacity to be really favored by God.

Exercise and Practice Your Faith

Blessings also come if we practice and exercise faith. We have to practice faith. We have to exercise our faith. We need to start practicing and continue to practice so we will begin to build up our capacity. Our capacity is just too shallow, too small. But when we exercise our faith, when we do our spiritual aerobics, we begin to build. When we study the Bible, when we read God's Word, when we meditate with God, when we praise God—all this builds up our capacity to receive the blessings of God.

A certain person went to heaven and was there complaining that he did not get the blessings on earth that he thought he deserved. God took him over in a corner and said, "See that blessing? That blessing had your name on it, but that blessing is in the deep water; your water's too shallow."

We have to push out into deep waters to really find favor with God. We can't stay in the shallow water and on the dock. We can't sit on the banks of life. We have to push out into the deep water where God can really bless us deeply.

Removing Cain from Self

Exercising and building up our capacity will help us rebuke the spirit of Cain in us. We all have a little of Cain in us, and we need to rebuke that spirit. We can't get excited when others are blessed. When someone is

sick, everybody visits. We don't have a problem dealing with people who are having problems. We are
there to minister to them. We'll take food to their
house. We will be there. We will be at the funeral. But
we can't rejoice when something good happens to
them.

That is the spirit of Cain in us. If we really want to
find favor with God, we have to get the Cain out of us.
We have to rebuke the Cain in us. We have to repent
and say, "Get out of here, Cain, get out of my life. I
don't want you in my life."

Serving Notice on Cain's Children

Also, in relationship to Cain, we have to serve notice
on Cain's children. If we really want to be blessed, we
have to tell the children of Cain that we're not scared
of them anymore. We can't be blessed because some of
us are literally scared of the children of Cain. We're
born with only two fears: the fear of loud noises and
the fear of falling. Those are the only two things a
baby fears. If we make a loud noise, babies will jump.
If we drop them, their eyes will get big. But they fear
nothing else. All other fears are learned.

For approximately the first twelve months of our
lives we were fearless. Because we have so many fears

now, we can hardly imagine ourselves fearless. The first twelve months of our lives we would put our hands in a dog's mouth. We would pull a cat's tail. If a rattlesnake came in the room, we would try to play with it. If a fire burned in the fireplace, we would put our hand in the fire.

But life has taught us some things. Experience has taught us that it doesn't make sense to put our hand in the fire. Also, Cain's children have been working on us and have taught us some things. Cain's children's criticism, rejection and ridicule have programmed us. Every time we advanced, Cain's children have rejected us. Cain's children have isolated us. Cain's children have talked about us.

We must tell Cain's children, "I don't care what you say about me and I don't care how you criticize me. You can't scare me because I want to be blessed by God. God has a blessing in store for me. Get out of here, Cain. Get out of my life."

Every time we get ready to bless somebody, Cain's children tell us to keep that blessing to ourselves. Cain tries to keep us greedy. Cain tries to keep us selfish. So, we need to serve notice to the spirit of Cain that he is no longer in control.

Every time we get ready to bless God with a praise, the Cains start looking at us, telling us we're just trying to show off. Sorry Cain. I will bless the Lord at all times. His praises will ever be on my lips. Bless the Lord, O my soul and all that is within me, bless His holy name.

Summary

If we want to be blessed and find favor with God and man, we must pay the price. There is a price tag on every blessing. Paying the price means accepting the responsibilities that inevitably come with blessings. Paying the cost of being blessed also means enduring the isolation, rejection and criticism of those who don't want us to be blessed, namely the descendants of Cain. These descendants of Cain think our blessings should have been their blessings.

To overcome the Cain Immunity Deficiency Syndrome (CIDS), we must 1) accept the responsibilities that come with blessings, 2) not be small-minded, 3) exercise and practice our faith, and 4) remove Cain from self and serve notice on his children that we are not scared of them anymore.

CHAPTER SEVEN

Blessed Through Humility

Matthew 5:3–12 (KJV)

3 *Blessed are the poor in spirit: for theirs is the kingdom of heaven.*

4 *Blessed are they that mourn: for they shall be comforted.*

5 *Blessed are the meek: for they shall inherit the earth.*

6 *Blessed are they which do hunger and thirst after righteousness: for they shall be filled.*

7 *Blessed are the merciful: for they shall obtain mercy.*

8 *Blessed are the pure in heart: for they shall see God.*

9 *Blessed are the peacemakers: for they shall be called the children of God.*

10 *Blessed are they which are persecuted for righteousness' sake: for theirs is the kingdom of heaven.*

11 *Blessed are ye, when men shall revile you, and persecute you, and shall say all manner of evil against you falsely, for my sake.*
12 *Rejoice, and be exceeding glad: for great is your reward in heaven: for so persecuted they the prophets which were before you.*

Jesus begins His sermon on the mountain by saying, *"Blessed are the poor in spirit: for theirs is the kingdom of heaven"* (v.3). I want to suggest that all the other Beatitudes grow out of this first one. In addition, humility is directly related to all the other Beatitudes, therefore we are blessed through humility.

I had the rare pleasure of being home on a recent Saturday afternoon. I turned on the television and Michigan was playing Notre Dame in one of the great classic football rivalries. With less then two minutes left in the game, Notre Dame took the lead. The player who caught the touchdown pass, drew attention to himself. There is a rule in college football that if you draw attention to yourself, your team will be penalized fifteen yards, so the referee threw the flag. Notre Dame lost the game. I submit that if that player had not drawn attention to himself, Notre Dame would have won rather than Michigan. Much like the referee in that game, God is throwing the flag on some of us. We are drawing attention to ourselves. And God, the

Great Referee, is throwing the flag on us and that is blocking our blessings.

Humility: Evasive and Demonstrated

Humility means getting down off of our high horses of pride and self-righteousness. Humility means getting down off of our high horse of thinking we are somebody outside of Christ. Humility means getting down off our high horse of all our degrees and achievements. Humility is so evasive that we think we have it when we actually don't.

> *God, the Great Referee, is throwing the flag on us and that is blocking our blessings.*

It's hard to be humble. Often I hear people say, "I'm humbled." Well, they *were* until they said it. Once they said it, humility went out the window. Humility is very evasive. Humility is demonstrated, not spoken. We can participate in events of humility. We demonstrate humility. Jesus said if they offer us the high seat, we should take the low seat. Then when we take the low seat, men will give us the high seat. That's a demonstration of humility. I'm thankful that God has blessed me in acts of humility. I dare not say that I'm humble because it will be gone.

An Old Testament Illustration

The Old Testament character, Naaman (2 Kings 5:1–14), had a problem getting down off of his high horse. Naaman was a great man, a valiant soldier, and highly regarded by men and God. But he had leprosy. The narrative tells us that a humble, little maiden girl from Irsael told Naaman's wife about a prophet named Elisha who could heal Naaman's leprosy.

So Naaman and his men rode up to the house of Elisha. But Elisha didn't come outside and Naaman wouldn't get off his high horse. In other words, Naaman was a highly regarded, valiant soldier; therefore, the man of God, Elisha, should come out to him. He should not

Humility is demonstrated, not spoken.

have to get off his high horse to knock on the door and ask somebody to heal him. Do you see Naaman's attitude?

The man of God sent a messenger out to Naaman. It angered Naaman that the man of God wouldn't come out. The messenger told Naaman to go wash seven times in the Jordan River and his flesh would be cleansed. But Naaman still couldn't get off his high horse. He said, "What do you mean, go and wash in the dirty Jordan River? Are not the rivers of where I come from in Damascus much cleaner than those of the dirty Jordan?"

Then a humble servant of Naaman told him, "My father, if the prophet told you to do this great thing you ought to do it." The story has a happy ending: Naaman got down from his high horse and washed not one time but seven times as the man of God had said. In obedience, he dipped himself seven times in the Jordan River and

God wants us to step down off our high horse.

when he came up, his skin was as clean as a young man's.

Some of us cannot be cleansed because we cannot get off our high horses. We cannot be obedient to what the Word of God is telling us. Many of us are still dealing with attitudes of self-sufficiency. God wants us to step down off of our high horse.

A Personal Testimony

Some years ago, I was invited to Alaska to lead a revival. While there, God spoke to me in the pulpit about a young lady for my son, George III, to marry. I wrestled with what I understood God to be saying. Finally, in obedience to what God was asking me to do, He asked me to claim it in His name. Six and a half years later, the couple walked down the aisle and was married. What is significant is how I got to Alaska. Who invited me there and why did they invite me? I didn't know the pastor there and I had never heard of him. When I got there, I asked him why he had invited me to come do this revival.

He told me, "Oh, I've been to your church. I was there and saw you carrying chairs with the men. I said to myself, 'If I were pastor of this church, I wouldn't carry chairs.' I decided you must be the man I want to run this revival." There would not have been a blessed wedding in my family if there had not been an act of humility on my part. There would not be a Spirit-filled daughter-in-law if not for an act of humility on my part.

Action Attitudes

These blessings in the text are commonly called the Beatitudes. They are really action attitudes. They are demonstrated attitudes. They are attitudes with a verb in front of them. These are "be-attitudes." These are acts of attitude that are put into a form of demonstration. The Beatitudes should really be interpreted not as receivers of the blessing, but as an inherent state of happiness. The receivers are just simply blessed.

Scripture tells us, beginning in Chapter 5, Jesus sees all these people who are not taking advantage of the abundant life the Father sent Him down to bring. Jesus says, "I came that you might have life and you might have it more abundantly, and look at you. You are no living abundantly." So, Jesus sets the disciples down and tells them how to be blessed. He didn't talk to the multitude. He set the disciples down and taught them how to be blessed. And He wants us, His contemporary disciples, to sit down and learn how to be blessed.

The Beatitudes—they are really action attitudes.

Blessed Are the Poor in Spirit

"Blessed are the poor in spirit: for theirs is the kingdom of heaven" (v.3). Jesus is not necessarily saying poor in material things. One can be rich, but poor in spirit; one can be poor, and poor in spirit. Jesus is saying that the poor in spirit know their help comes only from the Lord. Blessed are those that have a be-attitude: they are living in an inherent state of knowing that their help comes from the Lord. Blessed are those that are poor in spirit; they are blessed because they know they are nothing without God. I don't care how much money we have or how little money

we have, we are blessed because we realize we are nothing without God. We are but a ship without a sail.

Blessed Are They That Mourn

"Blessed are they that mourn: for they shall be comforted" (v.4). What do they mourn about? And who shall comfort them? They mourn about their past sins. They mourn about the sinful conditions of the world, and they mourn because they are truly sorry for their sinful life. They're not walking around with an attitude of I'm okay, you're okay. Their attitude is that I was born in sin and conceived in iniquity. Those who mourn are almost in a state of constant repentance. Every moment they are not reaching the holiness of God, they mourn about it. But, thank God, they hear the voice of Jesus saying, *"Come unto me, all ye that labour and are heavy laden, and I will give you rest"* (Matthew 11:28 - KJV).

Blessed are those that have a be-attitude: they are living in an inherent state of knowing that their help comes from the Lord.

Have we mourned this week for our past sins, our present sins, and our sinful condition? Some of us have been through a whole week thinking, "I'm okay."

"I'm okay" is opposite from a spirit of humility, and we are blessed through humility.

Blessed Are the Meek

"Blessed are the meek: for they shall inherit the earth" (v.5). Well, what does Jesus mean when He says meek? Is He talking about the wimps and the nerds of our society? I think not. Is He talking about those who are shy and those who are timid? I think not. These are types of natural meekness. Jesus is referring to a meekness that is grace meekness. Meekness is a fruit of the Spirit in the book of Galatians. God honors meekness.

> Those who mourn are almost in a state of constant repentance.

Meekness is great in the eyes of God. He says that those who are meek shall inherit the earth and they will find favor with man.

How do we know who's meek? What are the characteristics of one who has the grace of meekness? First, a meek person is patient with wrong—with wrong people, with wrong job situations, and even with wrong children. A meek person is always gentle even in the midst of wrong. A meek person does not lash out at others. A meek person does not cut others down. A meek person doesn't flare up and rip others apart, even if they are being ripped apart themselves. A meek person doesn't retaliate. That is grace, not natural meekness. A meek person who has grace meekness will not always expect to be treated with respect and reverence. A meek person who has grace meekness shall inherit the earth and shall find favor with others in the midst of violence and turmoil.

A meek person is always gentle even in the midst of wrong.

We see meekness in Jesus as he rode into Jerusalem on Palm Sunday on a lowly donkey. He rode meekly, humbly and lowly on a donkey. But He was not scared. He was not scared of the Pharisees, and He was not scared of the disciples. Meekness characterizes humility, and we are blessed through humility.

Blessed Are They That Hunger

"Blessed are they which do hunger and thirst after righteousness: for they shall be filled" (v.6). The Bible says those who are blessed most of the time feel deep down in their souls they want to be like Jesus. Those that are blessed hunger to be like Jesus. They realize they are not righteous in themselves; yet they hunger after righteousness. If we want to be blessed, we ought to thirst after righteousness. God has promised us that if

we hunger and thirst after His righteousness, we will be blessed. Seeking His righteousness with a hunger and a thirst is an act of humility, and we are blessed through humility.

Blessed Are the Merciful

James 5:11 says that the Lord is very pitiful and of tender mercy. In the past I was bothered when that word "pitiful" was used to describe the Lord. Don't let the word *pitiful* mislead you like it misled me. It means that God shows pity to everyone. His pity is wide and long. He shows pity

> Those that are blessed hunger to be like Jesus.

to the poor and, yes, even to the proud. He shows pity to those that are stuck up and those who are smart. He shows pity to the rich and to the poor. He shows pity to black people and to white people.

From pity springs mercy; and from mercy springs more mercy; and from more mercy springs blessings. So they are blessed who obtain mercy. It's a reflex action. Mercy goes out and mercy comes in. Mercy is like a new reflex action. Every time mercy hits, mercy flies up. It's like a boomerang. Mercy goes out; mercy comes back in. You throw mercy out, mercy returns.

Many of us have a hard time showing mercy. We even have a hard time showing mercy even to our own children. We should think about the mercy God gave us when we messed up. If we do, we may have a different attitude toward those we refuse to forgive or to have mercy or pity on. We should look back over our lives and see if our daughter or son is really worse than we were. Maybe he or she just got caught and we didn't. Blessed are the merciful for they shall obtain mercy. If we want to be blessed, we should show mercy like Jesus shows mercy.

From pity springs mercy; and from mercy springs more mercy; and from more mercy springs blessings.

Blessed Are the Pure in Heart

To be blessed, the heart must be cleansed of all carnal thinking. To be blessed, we must have a pure heart. We must have a clean heart so we can see God with an eye of faith. We need to flush out our hearts with repentance and confession. *"If we confess our sins, he is faithful and just to forgive us our sins, and to cleanse us from all unrighteousness"* (1 John 1:9 - KJV). That is a promise.

David said, *"Create in me a clean heart, O God; and renew a right spirit within me"* (Psalm 51:10 - KJV).

Why did David want a clean heart? He wanted a clean heart so he might see God. What we need is a heart laxative. We need to give our hearts an enema. We need to give our hearts some Ex-Lax or some Correctol. We need to give our hearts some prune juice to help us clean out all negative thinking.

Blessed Are the Peacemakers

"Blessed are the peacemakers: for they shall be called the children of God" (v.9). Jesus said these words in a time when men were warlike in Galilee. Jesus, in a midst of warlike attitudes, says, "Blessed are the peacemakers." However, things have not changed too much today. Men are still warlike and the world still values violence. Movie makers tell us that if they make a movie without violence, the movie will not sell. If nonviolent movies don't sell, that means violence is valued by the world. Yet Jesus looked over the multitude—those who go to work everyday with turmoil and violence in their homes, schools, and churches—and said, *"Blessed are the peacemakers: for they shall be called the children of God."*

What are some characteristics of a peacemaker? A peacemaker today is one who refuses to take sides in conversations related to relational conflicts. Peacemakers sometimes frustrate us when we try to tell them how somebody did us wrong. Peacemakers always find some possible truth to both sides of the story. Peacemakers realize there are two sides to every story and search for the other side of the story. They often frustrate us and sometimes make us mad. We want them to agree with us. Check out their lives and see how blessed they are. Peacemakers learn to roll with the punches; they prioritize for what they are willing to fight. They are great defenders of salvation and the gospel. Peacemakers exist in a state of happiness. We are blessed through the attitude of peacemakers.

> A peacemaker today is one who refuses to take sides in conversations related to relational conflicts.

Blessed Are They Which are Persecuted

"Blessed are they which are persecuted for righteousness' sake: for theirs is the kingdom of heaven" (v.10). The prophets were persecuted; Jesus was persecuted. We need to understand that if we stand up for righteousness, we will undergo some ridicule. If we refuse to engage in the office party's spiked punch at Christmas time, somebody will talk about us. If we save our body for marriage and don't engage in fornication, somebody will talk about us. If we hold up the name

of Jesus, somebody will talk about us. If we give expressive praise, even in church, somebody will call us a fanatic. If we try to do right on our job, if we don't cuss with the guys, if we don't engage in gossip, and if we don't engage in conversations about relational conflict, somebody will persecute us. However, we have the sweet assurance that if we are persecuted for trying to be righteous, we have the promise of being blessed, even in persecution.

> *If we stand up for righteousness, we will undergo some ridicule.*

The Way Up Is Down

Lowliness is the path to holiness and holiness is the path to blessedness. The way up is down. Blessed are they that mourn. We cannot mourn without appreciating how insufficient we are to handle life in our own strength. That's humility. The way up, without question, is the way down. Blessed are the meek.

But we cannot be meek without humility. The way up is down. Blessed are those who hunger after righteousness for they shall be filled. They are filled because they are empty. We cannot hunger after righteousness if we're proud and self-righteous and too proud to beg. We beg Him, "Spirit of the living God, fall fresh on me. Mold me, melt me, break me, but whatever You do, fill me." A spiritual appetite cannot be satisfied unless we have humility. The way up is down.

Jesus demonstrated that the way up is down when He got down and washed the disciples' feet (John 13:4–15). The disciples came in off the dusty roads of Palestine. While they argued about who was greatest, who would sit on His right side, and who would sit on the left side, Jesus said, "Let Me teach you a lesson for all times." He took a towel and started washing their feet. When He came to Peter, he said, "No Lord, You can't wash my feet." Peter had a problem with humility because Peter didn't want to have to wash anybody else's feet.

Lowliness is the path to holiness and holiness is the path to blessedness. The way up is down.

Some of us wouldn't want anybody to wash our feet because we don't ever want to have to wash anybody else's feet. However, this is one of Peter's repenting moments. Jesus said, "If I do not wash you, you have no part with Me." Peter repented and said, "Lord, not my feet only, but also my hands and my head!"

We need to repent when we realize that the way up is down. After washing the disciples feet, Jesus said, "Do you know what I've done for you? The servant is not greater than his lord. You called Me Master and I am. If I can get down on My knees and wash your feet, you ought to wash one another's feet. Now, do you know what I've done? If you know these things, then blessed, happy are they that do them."

This is not the only time that Jesus demonstrated that the way up is down because when He died on Calvary, He went down in a grave. He went way down. He went down a little farther into the depths of hell to set the captives free. He went down, but early Sunday morning He got up. He went down in humility, but got up with all power in His hands.

If we can go down in humility, we can come up blessed. Those that humble themselves will be exalted before God and man.

Summary

Jesus' Sermon on the Mount, referred to as the Be-attitudes, teaches us valuable lessons relative to how to be blessed through humility. The Be-attitudes are attitudes of humility demonstrated. Humility must be demonstrated and is very evasive. The first Be-attitude, *Blessed are the Poor in Spirit*, encompasses the basic theme of all the other Be-attitudes, that is, those that demonstrate attitudes of humility are blessed.

Each of the nine Beatitudes is characterized by humility. Happy and blessed are they that demonstrate these characteristics of humility. However, humility is evasive, so we the believers should work on constantly demonstrating humility as characterized in the Sermon on the Mount. Jesus teaches us a great lesson in humility when He washed the disciples' feet. He concluded this act by saying, *"Happy are you if you do this"* (John 13:17 - KJV). In other words, blessed are those who practice humility. We can be indeed blessed through humility.

CHAPTER EIGHT

Blessed Through Trials and Tribulations

James 1:12 (NIV)

12 *Blessed is the man who perseveres under trial, because when he has stood the test, he will receive the crown of life that God has promised to those who love him.*

Blessed is the man who endures to the end, who perseveres under trial. When it's all over, when he has stood the test, he will receive the crown of life that God has promised to those who love Him.

Blessed on the Other Side of Through

Are you going *through* anything? Have you ever been *through* something? You're probably in one of three positions: you're in it; you're going into it; or, praise God, you're through it.

James, the earthly half brother of our Lord and Savior Jesus Christ, says to us "*when* we fall into trials and tribulations," not *if* we fall into trials and tribulations. The explicit suggestion is that we *will* have trials and tribulations. They will come in divergent forms, in different and various ways: sickness, disease, accidents, disappointments, sorrow, suffering and even death. We need to know that blessed is the man and woman who make it through, for there is a blessing on the other side of through.

> Being tried, results in patience and patience means perseverance, and perseverance brings us into perfection.

Are you experiencing any sickness? Get through. Are you experiencing any sorrow? Get through. Are you experiencing any suffering? Get through. Have you had any disappointments recently? Just get through. Have you had any oppression, depression, or suppression? Get through. There is a blessing on the other side of through.

Tribulation = Perseverance = Perfection

This is a great lesson on endurance. Testing, or being tried, results in patience and patience means perseverance, and perseverance brings us into perfection. God allows us to be tried and tested because it results in perseverance.

The King James Version calls it patience, which means perseverance. It's necessary to have perseverance to come into completion or into perfection. Just as a child must persevere to come into maturity so must the believer.

We will have trials and tribulations.

God allows testing in our lives that results in patience or perseverance, and perseverance matures us into perfection.

Yes, God allows testing, yet we must not mistake God's allowing us to be tested with God tempting us. God does not tempt us. That would be against the nature of God. God does not tempt us to do evil. Evil results from our own lusts. The word "temptation" used in the King James Version has two meanings. One is "testing for righteousness." The other meaning is "enticement to sin." There are two meanings in the Greek for "testing," and they're used interchangeably.

In the context of James 1:2–12, the meaning is not about enticement to sin, but about testing for righteousness; testing that makes us stronger.

Overload Principle

Many of us today are exercising for health; we're jogging to overload our heart. It's called the overload principle. If we increase our heart rate, depending upon our age, for about twenty minutes it will help our heart get stronger. If we lift weights, the muscle, when it is overloaded, gets stronger. And if we do many repetitions, it will build up our endurance. We overload our physical bodies to become stronger.

Overloading works mentally, also. The more we read, the better we read. We can learn to speed-read by overloading ourselves. When we overload, we become stronger and we learn to endure, which will help bring us into completion or perfection.

God is the originator of the overload principle. God is the author of what we see people do now for their physical bodies and their mental bodies. Similarly, God permits overload sometimes, but the overload is just to make us stronger. Through the trials and tribulations and temptations of sickness, suffering, disappointment, oppression, depression, and even death, we get overloaded to become stronger so we can make it to the other side of through.

Ask for Wisdom

The first step in getting through is to ask God for wisdom (James 1:5). God will give it to us generously without scolding us for asking. We are scared to ask God because we figure we've been a Christian for ten or twenty years, and we ought to already know. We judge ourselves and say, "I've been coming to church for twenty years and Sunday School for ten years and I shouldn't have to ask God for that."

We get overloaded to become stronger so we can make it to the other side of through.

God said, "No, just come and ask me. I won't say I already told you so." When we ask each other something a second time, we usually answer, "Didn't I just tell you that once?" We may think God is like us humans, so we're scared to go back and ask Him again. We're scared we will hear Mama's voice or Daddy's voice saying, "I told you that three times." God won't say that. So if any man lacks wisdom, let him ask. God won't scold, criticize, or judge us, but will give it to us generously.

Understand that we are referring to wisdom, not knowledge. Knowledge is good, but it won't get us to the other side of through. Part of wisdom is knowing what God is doing to us in the midst of trials and tribulations. Knowledge won't really teach us that. Knowledge may know what is true, but wisdom knows the truth. Wisdom is more than knowledge.

> *Part of wisdom is knowing what God is doing to us in the midst of trials and tribulations.*

Wisdom prepares us deep in our soul to understand that when we are going through something, God is working with us and strengthening us. We think God is beating up on us, but He is really just strengthening us. He's really preparing us. He wants us to have some perseverance. He wants us to be able to endure. If we want this wisdom, we must ask for it, God won't fuss. He'll give us this wisdom generously. He won't just give us a little bit, He'll give us abundant wisdom.

Count It All Joy

How do we get through? First, we ask God for wisdom. Second, we count it all joy (James 1:2). What?

Count it all joy? God, are you serious? God is saying, "Oh yes, count it all joy and rejoice in the status of where we are. In sickness, count it all joy. In suffering, count it all joy. In disappointments, count it all joy. In sorrow, rejoice and count it all joy. In trouble, count it all joy."

Can we really count it all joy? Counting it all a joy is our ticket through. It is the way through. We may have known some people who didn't make it through. They would have made it through whatever they were dealing with if they had counted it all joy. Making it through requires an attitude of joy. It requires a spirit of joy. It requires us to change our attitude from negative thinking to positive thinking.

Counting it all a joy is our ticket through.

When I recently sponsored a tour to West Africa, we visited three countries: Gambia, Senegal, and Ghana. While in Ghana, I was invited to preach at a church in Accra. It was obvious from the general surroundings that the people had so very little materially. Yet, they were rejoicing in the midst of it. They literally danced in the aisles when they gave their offerings in church. I preached from James 1:2 from the King James Version, "Count It All Joy." I clearly realized that I was preaching to myself, just looking at the congregation there. I was preaching to them, but I received a sermon in action from them.

Picture Your Paycheck

If we want to get through, we should 1) ask for wisdom, 2) count it all joy, and 3) remember what our paycheck is going to look like, doing that always helped me when I was working. Somehow, it just helped me get through the week if I knew that Saturday the boss would pay me a nice paycheck. I've been on jobs where I was ready to walk off, but I thought about my paycheck. I decided to stay till Saturday just to get my check.

As we go through trials, we need to keep our eyes on the blessing, keep our eyes on the prize, and keep our eyes and our hearts on the reward because there is a blessing at the end of through. At the end of through there is a crown. The crown is eternal, everlasting, and glorious.

The Problem of Double-mindedness

To make sure that we can get through, we need to understand a problem is involved. Our problem is that we are double-minded. *"But when he asks, he must believe and not doubt, because he who doubts is like a wave of the sea, blown and tossed by the wind. That man (or that woman) should not think he will receive anything from the Lord; he is a double-minded man, unstable in all he does"* (James 1:6-8 - NIV).

A double-minded person is always beginning something, stopping something, starting all over again. A double-minded person is unstable, wavering, tossed to and fro, just like the wind. He or she has a faith that's shaky, flaky, and raggedy. He or she is always picking it up and putting it down.

The wonderful thing about being blessed through trials is that it is based on a promise of God. Remember what we used to say when we were young and wanted to get things from our parents? We would say, "You promised?" We asked, "Daddy, will you take me to the ball game? Daddy, do you promise?" If we could just get Daddy to say, "Yes, I promise," then we could go back to bed because Daddy promised. Sometimes our earthly Daddy may let us down, but we have a Heavenly Father who is the author of promise-keepers. He has kept every promise that He has ever made. We don't have to ask Him, "Daddy, do you promise?" He has already promised that there is a blessing on the other side of through. God promises that we can be blessed through trials and tribulations.

Summary

God has promised that if we get through our trials and tribulations, there is a blessing awaiting us. Trials are overcome through perseverance, and perseverance brings us into perfection. The process can be compared to the overload principle used in physical fitness training. When we overload a muscle through the use of exercise, we increase the strength of that muscle. Likewise, when God overloads us with trials and tribulations, we grow stronger.

To get through our trials and tribulations, we are admonished to 1) ask for wisdom, 2) count it all joy, and 3) picture our paycheck.

In addition, to receive this blessing we must overcome the problem of being double- minded. Because God is the first and greatest promise-keeper, we have the assurance that we can be blessed through trials and tribulations.

Blessed Through Blessing God's Leader

(The Church Victorious)

Exodus 17:5–16 (KJV)

5 And the LORD said unto Moses, Go on before the people, and take with thee of the elders of Israel; and thy rod, wherewith thou smotest the river, take in thine hand, and go.

6 Behold, I will stand before thee there upon the rock in Horeb; and thou shalt smite the rock, and there shall come water out of it, that the people may drink. And Moses did so in the sight of the elders of Israel.

7 And he called the name of the place Massah, and Meribah, because of the chiding of the children of Israel, and because they tempted the LORD, saying, Is the LORD among us, or not?

8 Then came Amalek, and fought with Israel in Rephidim.

9 And Moses said unto Joshua, Choose us out men, and go out, fight with Amalek: to morrow I will stand on the top of the hill with the rod of God in mine hand.

10 So Joshua did as Moses had said to him, and fought with Amalek: and Moses, Aaron, and Hur went up to the top of the hill.

11 And it came to pass, when Moses held up his hand, that Israel prevailed: and when he let down his hand, Amalek prevailed.

12 But Moses' hands were heavy; and they took a stone, and put it under him, and he sat thereon; and Aaron and Hur stayed up his hands, the one on the one side, and the other on the other side; and his hands were steady until the going down of the sun.

13 And Joshua discomfited Amalek and his people with the edge of the sword.

14 And the LORD said unto Moses, Write this for a memorial in a book, and rehearse it in the ears of Joshua: for I will utterly put out the remembrance of Amalek from under heaven.

15 And Moses built an altar, and called the name of it Jehovah-nissi:

16 For he said, Because the LORD hath sworn that the LORD will have war with Amalek from generation to generation.

A point of clarification is necessary because too many of us only think of money when we hear the word "blessing." We live in America, this money-driven society, so when we hear blessing, we can't hear anything but money.

But blessings come in various ways. There are many kinds of blessings. This particular scripture deals with the blessing of a victorious life. So whatever battle we may be in, or whatever situation we need victory in, this scripture applies to us. This Old Testament scripture tells us how the people of God supported Pastor Moses by lifting up his tired, weary, heavy arms in battle, and God gave the people a blessing of victory.

> *Because the people supported the arms of the leader, God gave them the victory.*

Because the people supported the arms of the leader, God gave them the victory. There is a blessing in the leader. Bless the leader and be blessed.

Background

This text takes place during the forty-year wilderness journey. God had brought His people out of the bondage and slavery from Egypt. But they complained against Pastor Moses and accused him of bringing them too far too fast. Does that sound a little familiar to us? Hard times fell upon them, and they had no water. They told Pastor Moses that they should have stayed in bondage. You should have kept us in bondage. You should have let us stay back in Egypt. You should have let us stay in slavery. It would have been better for us to be back in slavery drinking vinegar water rather than being out here headed for the Promised Land with no water at all. They accused Pastor Moses of setting them free, and by setting them free they had too much responsibility. They said that if all this is required, we would rather not be blessed.

Blessings Carry Responsibilities

Many of us believers are saying today that "if." If I have to go to Sunday School, Bible study, and Discipleship Training, and tithe my money, I would rather not be blessed. If I have to spend energy praising the Lord and wearing out my knees praying to the Lord, I would rather not be blessed. If I have to stand on my feet to give God some praise, if it costs all this, I would just rather not be blessed.

The Journey

Pastor Moses has been instructed to lead, to go before the people, and take some of the elders and the deacons with him. The Lord said to him, take thy rod and strike the rock. He struck the rock and water came out of the rock and the people drank. He called the place Massah and Meribah because Massah means tempted or tested, and Meribah rebelliousness or strife. He called it that because this was the place where they lost faith. This was the place where they got stuck on the way. This was the place where they became stunted. This was the place where they began to question whether the Lord was with them or not. Amalek comes up against them. Amalek, a descendant of Esau, attacks God's people. Pastor Moses chooses the young man named Joshua to lead the army. You will remember that Joshua, forty years later, will lead the people across the Jordan River into the Promised Land. Look at God preparing Joshua to be the new pastor. Joshua was doing his OJT (on-the-job training). Moses said to Joshua, you take them in to fight the battle, but I will go up on the mountain. I will fix my eyes upon the hills from whence cometh our help. So Pastor Moses goes up on the mountain with rod and staff in hand. The Bible says that as long as Pastor Moses lifted up his hands the people of God were winning. But when Moses dropped down his hands, the Amalekites were winning. Lifted hands in prayer and praise brought the victory. But dropped hands brought defeat. We have heard over and over again that there is power in prayer and praise. Uplifted hands, power and victory. Dropped down hands, no power and defeat. Get the picture. Uplifted hands, we win, and dropped hands, we lose.

A problem occurred. Pastor Moses got tired. Pastor Moses' arms grew tired and weary. Pastor Moses could no longer lift up his hands. Surely defeat was on the way. But help was also on the way. Aaron, the brother of Moses, and Hur, the brother-in-law of Moses, got a stone or rock and propped Moses up from behind. Moses sat on the rock.

Lifted up hands in prayer and praise brought the victory. But dropped down hands brought defeat.

They came along beside Moses and held up Moses' arms. They supported Moses' arms. They kept his arms lifted up until the sun went down. They kept his arms lifted up until the victory was won. Notice, they lifted his arms up. They supported Moses. They did not try to take the rod from Moses. They did not try to take the leadership from Moses. They could have said, "But Moses you are too tired, let me lead." They could have said, "But Moses you are too old, let me lead." They could have said, "But Moses you didn't know what you were doing in the first place. I am the one that really should be leading this congregation." They could have said all these things. But no, they supported the Pastor. They lifted him up. They blessed him. There is a blessing in lifting up the leader. Wherever we go, it doesn't matter what church or who the pastor is, there is a blessing in blessing the leader. We ought to always support the leader. We ought to always support the vision. We ought to always support the ministry. Wherever we go, let it be known that God's Word says that there is a blessing in blessing the leader.

Sometimes the leader gets weak. The leader may not always be able to lead us in praise. The leader may not always be able to do a holy dance. The leader may not always be able to run a victory lap. Somebody might have to run a victory lap for the leaders.

> It doesn't matter what church or who the pastor is, there is a blessing in blessing the leader.

Keep on praying for our leaders. Keep on praising God for our leader. Notice that they propped Moses up as he sat on a stone or a rock. They gave him a rock to sit on. The rock is the Word of God. Jesus is the Rock. He is the chief cornerstone. Paul says no other foundation can be laid other than Jesus Christ. The songwriter said, "Be very sure your anchor grips the solid rock." This rock is Jesus. He is the One. We must support the leader with the Word of God. We must be rooted in the Word. We must go to discipleship training. We must be a disciple. It is not enough just to be a Christian, we also need to be a disciple. We must support the leader with discipleship and support the leader with prayer. We must support the leader with the gift of the Spirit and with the fruit of the Spirit, and be blessed.

Memorize the Blessing (Victory)

After the victory was won God said, rehearse this day into the mind and ears of Joshua. Just like a record, play it back. God said, I especially want Joshua to remember this day. Then Moses built an altar and named the place Jehovah-nissi, which means the Lord is my banner. Then He says that Amalek will always be with us until we get to heaven. This is a picture of the church and the believer in spiritual warfare. This is a picture of the church, victorious, yes, but a church and its believers who are in spiritual warfare. Amalek, like Esau, represents flesh. This is a picture of the Old Testament wilderness that represents our wilderness experience today. For we wrestle not against flesh and blood, but we wrestle against spirits in high places. Paul puts it this way in the New Testament. *"For the flesh lusts*

Our flesh today is too weak to overcome evil.

against the Spirit and the Spirit against the flesh. These are contrary one to the other" (Gal. 5:17 - KJV)

Spirit vs. Flesh

I want you to know that there is a battle going on. There is a war going on in you and in me where the Spirit wrestles against the flesh. And the flesh wrestles against the Spirit. The two are contrary one to the other. That is what makes the book I authored entitled *Praising the Hell Out of Yourself* so meaningful. The flesh

> As long as we live, we need to walk in the Spirit and not in the flesh.

fights against the Spirit and the Spirit fights against the flesh. Just like in the days of the Old Testament, God's people did not have the power to overcome Amalek on their own, that is, in the flesh.

Just like them, our flesh today is too weak to overcome evil. We cannot overcome evil in the flesh. God says Amelek will be with us from generation to generation. Therefore, as long as we live, we need to walk in the Spirit and not in the flesh. We cannot overcome our wilderness experiences in the flesh. We cannot overcome our secret addictions in the flesh. We cannot overcome the battle that we may be having with pornography, made available to us over the Internet, in the flesh. We cannot overcome the battle with masturbation in the flesh. We cannot overcome the battle with fornication in the flesh. We cannot overcome the battle with adultery in the flesh. We cannot overcome the battle with alcohol in the flesh. We cannot overcome the battle with nicotine in the flesh. We cannot overcome the battle with gambling in the flesh. We can't overcome the battle with overeating in the flesh. There is a drug in our society called food that is killing as many of us as crack cocaine. We cannot overcome that battle in the flesh. Amelek is too strong. But I have some good news. If we walk in the Spirit, keep holding up the bloodstained banner, and keep our hands lifted up to the hills, as long as we lift Him up, we win. But when the hands come down we lose. Not by our power, nor by might, but by the Spirit of the Lord.

The Victory Belongs to God

The victory belongs to God. This nomadic group of people had no training in warfare. As a matter of fact, this was the very first time they ever had to go to war. There is no evidence that they had great numbers. There is no evidence at all that they had any armor or any weapons. The only weapon they had was the weapon of the Spirit. The only weapon they had was prayer and praise. They lifted up praise and prayer. The victory did not belong to Pastor Moses, Joshua, Aaron, or to Hur. The victory did not belong to the people or to the congregation. The victory belonged to the Lord. Sometimes we get confused. Every time we have a little success, we think that we did it. But God did it. Whenever the Lord allows me to get around to writing a book on the life and blessing of the Greenforest Community Baptist Church, I know the title of the book already. The title of the book will be *God Did It.* God did it. From twenty-five to six thousand active members, God did it. Twenty-five hundred in Sunday School, God did it. Twelve million dollars combined budgets, God did it. Second largest African American Academy in the whole world, God did it. Eight million dollar day care center, God did it. We need to understand that all our success, accomplishments, and achievements belong to God. We are blessed! The victory is not ours, but the victory belongs to the Lord.

Fighting From a Blessing vs. Fighting For a Blessing

We need to understand that if we are going to be blessed and victorious, we must realize that we are not fighting *for* a blessing, we are fighting *from* a blessing. The victory has already been won. Too many of us are fighting for the victory rather than from the victory. Pastor Moses told Joshua, you go and do the fighting while I go up on the mountain. I will go up on the hill from whence cometh our help.

The victory is not ours, but the victory belongs to the Lord.

Pastor Moses said we are not fighting for the victory—we already have the victory as long as we can hold up the blood-stained banner. If perchance, I grow a little weary, hold up my arms. Prop up my arms. Set me upon the rock. Set me upon the Word of God.

The Power and Value of Remembering

Moses memorialized the victory by calling it Jehovah-nissi, which means the Lord is my banner. Then he said rehearse it in the ear of Joshua. I don't want Joshua to forget this moment. Forty years later, Joshua knew that God could push back the Jordan River because Moses had set it to his memory. Joshua, like Moses, after he crossed the Jordan River, set twelve stones. Why did he set the twelve stones? Joshua said, "So that when your children ask, you can tell them that it is the Lord who has brought us."

We are guilty of forgetting the God who gave us the victory. Recently I had to repent for not memorializing my grandson's healing blessing. My grandson had a perpetual cough or bark that the doctors could not diagnose or cure. We brought him to the church. We layed hands on him, put oil on him, and prayed for him. The doctors didn't know what to do and had given up. Yet, God healed him. I need to rehearse that in his ear. I need to tell my grandson, like a broken record, "Grandson when you were ten years old you had an affliction. You had an illness that the doctors couldn't cure. But God!" We have not rehearsed

> *We are guilty of forgetting the God who gave us the victory.*

this enough. He might forget it and lose the value of the blessing. But I have repented. Now I'm going to tell him every time I see him or think about it. It was God that blessed you. The reason that you are not coughing today, not barking today, and can go to school today is that God healed you. Maybe forty years down the line, maybe twenty-one years down the line, he may be in a wilderness himself, but he might remember that Grandy told me that the same God that healed me when I was ten years old can heal me today.

Stay Under the Banner

Whatever we do, we must stay under the banner. Jehovah-nissi means the Lord is my banner. It means the

Lord is my warrior. It means the Lord is my protector. We must stay under the banner. As long as we are under the banner, everything will be all right. But if we are over the banner, then the enemy can attack us. But if the banner is held up, we will have the victory. We must stay under the banner. If we are under the banner, the pastor's arms must be lifted up and victory belongs to the Lord. If the pastor's arms get a little tired, we must bless the pastor by propping him with the Word of God and holding his arms up. If we bless him, we will be blessed. There is a blessing in blessing the leader.

Summary

We can be blessed by blessing God's leader. In Exodus 17:5–16, the people of God were blessed with a victory over their enemy because they blessed the man of God by supporting him when he grew tired and weary. Blessings carry responsibilities. When we live up to our responsibility of supporting God's leader, God gives us the blessing of victorious living. This cannot be done in the flesh, but it can be accomplished in the Spirit. Therefore, the victory is not ours, but the victory belongs to the Lord. Remember that because the victory belongs to the Lord, we are fighting *from* a blessing rather than *for* a blessing. We are reminded to always remember past victories by rehearsing them and always staying under the protective banner of the Lord. We must bless the leader and be blessed.

CHAPTER TEN

Blessed Through Blunders

Romans 8:28 (KJV)

28 And we know that all things work together for good to them that love God, to them who are the called according to his purpose.

History records many incidents of how blessings came from blunders. One of the most notable ones is the story of Ivory soap—the floating soap. What happened was that the man who was making the soap forgot to turn the heat off. Rather than admitting his mistake, he went to lunch. Later he just shipped the batch out anyway. As it turned out, it was discovered that at that heat and temperature, soap would float. Now we have Ivory, the floating soap. It was a mistake. It was an accident. It was a blunder.

A blunder is a mistake that is made even though there were good intentions. For those of us who have ever made a blunder, I have some good news. God says, "All things work together for good to them that love God and are the called according to His purpose." Not everything is good. But all things work together for good. There is a difference. There are some things that are not good. It is not good that people get killed in car accidents. It is not good that tires blow out and cause cars to overturn, and people are maimed and injured. It is not good that people are addicted to alcohol and drugs. It is not good that people die of diseases, heart attacks, and the like. It is not good that a job is lost that is needed. It is not good that a child may be in jail.

> A blunder is a mistake that is made even though there were good intentions.

Also, all people are not good. There may be some good in all people, but there are some bad people. I have met some mean people. There are some low-down, evil, mean, bad people. So all things are not good and all people are not good. But God says that all things work together for good to those who love Him and are the called according to His purpose.

Spiritual Nearsightedness

Our problem is one of nearsightedness. We can see only what is right in front of us. God is saying not only do we need to see what is right in front of us, but we also need to see the end. We must position ourselves spiritually to see God working out the end results of our blunders before we get to the end. And God provides some provisions while He works it out. However, we do have some

> *Not everything is good. But all things work together for good.*

responsibility in the process. God wants to and is able to work it out. But He says that ALL works together for good to them who love Him and are the called according to His purpose. Loving Him and being called according to His purpose are our responsibilities in the process.

We need a visit to the Spiritual Optometrist (eye doctor). We need our spiritual lenses corrected. We are not to be nearsighted. We need to look beyond what is in front of us, to see what God has for us. God is our Spiritual Optometrist, our eye doctor. For He has the greatest vision and plan for our lives. He wants to take us along the journey of His vision. The problem is that we are looking down at where we are rather than looking up to where God wants to take us. God is calling us to look up. Look up to the hills from whence cometh our help. Look up to the Spirit that is our Counselor. Look up and get ready to be blessed. Do not be deceived, for God is not mocked.

We mustn't grow weary in doing good.

Let us not grow weary in good works, for in due season we will reap if we faint not. Don't lose heart. Look up, due season is on the way. Today may not be our due season, but due season may be tomorrow. Due season is right around the corner. Due season is next in line. We must hold on for due season.

Our Responsibilities

If we want God to work it out, here is what we must do. First of all, we mustn't grow weary in doing good. When bad things happen, and bad people come up against us, we cannot grow weary in doing good. It is hard, sometimes, to do good when bad things are happening to us. It is hard to treat people right when people are treating us wrong. Often we grow weary in doing good. We cannot get tired of doing good. When people aren't treating us right, we must keep on doing good. When people talk about us, we must keep on doing good. Why? Because God is working it out. When they scandalize our name, we must keep on doing good. When they overlook us for a promotion, we must keep on doing good. Even if we are laid off, we must keep on doing good. If our spouse walks out on us, we must keep on doing good. We cannot grow weary in doing good because God is able, and God will work it out.

> If we want God to work it out is to trust in the reliability of God's word and His promise.

A second thing we must do if we want God to work it out is to trust in the reliability of God's Word and His promise. We sing about it, "I will trust in the Lord." But do we really trust Him to work it out? We must trust in the reliability of His Word. His Word is His promise, and His promise is His Word. His Word says that all things work together for good to those who love Him and are the called according to His purpose. That is His Word and His promise. Trust in His promise. If we really trust Him, we can develop a "well, whatever" attitude. In the drama presentation, *"Praising the Hell Out of Yourself,"* there is a classic line. The line comes when the mother of this uppity neurosurgeon says, "My son is the head Negro surgeon." He promptly and properly corrects her, "Neuro, Neurosurgeon, mother, not Negro." And she says, "Well, whatever." If we trust in the Lord, we can develop a "well, whatever" attitude with evil and the devil. When the evil one comes up against us, if we trust in the Lord, we can say, "Well, whatever." When bad things happen to us, we can say, "Well, whatever." When bad people come up against us, we can say, "Well, whatever." Whatever comes up against us, if we trust in the Lord and trust in His promise, we can say, "Well, whatever" because we know that He is able to work it out, and He has promised in His Word that all things work together for good. The kids may be acting a little crazy now, but all things work together for good to those who love the Lord and are the called according to His purpose.

> If we really trust Him, we can develop a "well, whatever" attitude.

Third, it is our responsibility to make sure that we are called according to His purpose. All things work together for good to those who love the Lord and are the called according to His purpose. So if we want God to work it out, we need to make sure we are operating according to His purpose. What is His purpose? His purpose is very clear in the Bible. Luke's gospel makes it so simple: The Son of man came to seek and to save which simply means that if we are not seeking and trying to get people saved, we are not on His agenda. If we are not on His agenda, then whose agenda are we on? Christians need to stop playing church. We must do more than just come to church. Between Sundays we have to be Christians. Between Sundays we have to be on God's agenda. So wherever we go, we need to be seeking to make sure that everybody we meet is saved. When we go to the restaurant, we need to make sure that the waiter or waitress is saved. We need to ask them, "Are you saved?" We need to see everybody we meet as having a big "L" (for lost) on his/her forehead. Everybody has an "L" on his/her head until there is an "S" (for saved) on his/her head. That is His purpose—salvation. People ask me all the time, what is His will in my life? That's a good question. But first we need to deal with His will for ALL Christians. There is no need to focus on God's personal will for our lives until we are united in what God's will is for ALL Christians. In Ephesians 5:17–18 (KJV), He makes it very clear, *"Wherefore be ye not unwise, but understanding what the will of the Lord is. And be not drunk with wine, wherein is excess; but be filled with the Spirit."* The will of God is not that we are drunk with wine, but that we are filled with the Holy Spirit. This text is not referring to individual

> It is our responsibility to make sure that we are called according to His purpose.

spiritual gifts. Rather, it is dealing with Christian duties. As we are going, we will be filled. A filled person will have good intentions in his heart. Remember that good intentions are necessary for blunders to become blessings. If we want God to work it out be ye ever filled all the time. This is the will of God for all Christians. Another will of God for all Christians is given to us in the book of Thessalonians. *"Rejoice evermore. Pray without ceasing. In every thing give thanks: for this is the will of God in Christ Jesus concerning you"* (1 Thessalonians 5:16–18 - KJV). That is a Christian duty. God wants us to rejoice always and give thanks in everything. It may not be an easy thing to do, but if we want God to work it out we must rejoice always and give thanks. If the devil attacks us, we must rejoice and give thanks. If bad people come up against us, we must rejoice and give thanks. If our bodies are racked with pain, we must rejoice and give thanks. If our children don't want to act right, we must rejoice and give thanks. If bad news comes, we must rejoice and give thanks. Why rejoice? Rejoice because we are standing on His promise that all things work together for good to those who love the Lord and are the called according to His purpose.

> *Remember that good intentions are necessary for blunders to become blessings.*

Finally, if we want God to work it out, we must love Him. Love Him for who He is. Love Him for His goodness. Love Him for what He has done, what He is doing, and what He is going to do. For all things work together for good to those who love Him. The question is, do we love Him? We may blunder, but if we love Him, He will work it out. Peter blundered when he denied Christ, but God blessed Him with restoration by the Sea of Galilee. God worked it out. Jonah blundered when he took a ship to Tarshish, but God blessed him when he got to Ninevah. God worked it out. Paul blundered in his persecutions of Christians, but God blessed him on the Damascus Road. Adam blundered in the Garden of Eden, but God

If we want God to work it out, we must love Him.

sent a second Adam in Jesus who has blessed us. Pilate blundered when he released Barabbas, but early Sunday morning Jesus blessed when He got up out of the grave. God is still in the blessing business, and He specializes in turning blunders into blessings.

Summary

A blunder is a mistake made when we have good intentions. God has promised in His Word that He can bless us through our blunders. Romans 8:28, assures us of this promise. The reason we are not blessed through our blunders is that we suffer from spiritual nearsightedness. We focus on the immediate, and God wants us to be able to see the end. We must look up to God to help us correct our spiritual lenses so we can see what God has for us. God will turn a blunder into a blessing in due season, but we must hold on until our due season comes. Although God promises "all things work together for good to those who love Him and are the called according to His purpose," yet included are some provisions that are our responsibility. These responsibilities are: 1) do not grow weary in doing good, especially when bad things happen; 2) trust in the reliability of God's promise; 3) be called according to His purpose; and 4) love Him. God wants to and is able to bless us through our blunders.

CHAPTER ELEVEN

Blessed Through His Poorness

2 Corinthians 8:1–9 (KJV)

¹ Moreover, brethren, we do you to wit of the grace of God bestowed on the churches of Macedonia;

² How that in a great trial of affliction the abundance of their joy and their deep poverty abounded unto the riches of their liberality.

³ For to their power, I bear record, yea, and beyond their power they were willing of themselves;

⁴ Praying us with much entreaty that we would receive the gift, and take upon us the fellowship of the ministering to the saints.

⁵ *And this they did, not as we hoped, but first gave their own selves to the Lord, and unto us by the will of God.*

⁶ *Insomuch that we desired Titus, that as he had begun, so he would also finish in you the same grace also.*

⁷ *Therefore, as ye abound in every thing, in faith, and utterance, and knowledge, and in all diligence, and in your love to us, see that ye abound in this grace also.*

⁸ *I speak not by commandment, but by occasion of the forwardness of others, and to prove the sincerity of your love.*

⁹ *For ye know the grace of our Lord Jesus Christ, that, though he was rich, yet for your sakes he became poor, that ye through his poverty might be rich."*

Two basic spiritual propositions undergird this chapter: 1) we are blessed by Jesus' poorness, and 2) our stewardship should be like Jesus' stewardship. Take notice: *"For ye know the grace of our Lord Jesus Christ, that, though he was rich, yet for your sakes he became poor, that ye through his poverty might be rich"* (v.9).

A Stewardship Admonition

This is Paul speaking to the church at Corinth and to us. God speaks to us through Paul speaking to the church at Corinth. Paul encourages them to give liberally and generously to the poor home church at Jerusalem based upon the liberal, generous giving of the poor churches in the Macedonia area. A famine had fallen upon Jerusalem and though they were the home, parent church, they were in need of financial support. So Paul makes a visit to Corinth and tells them about the churches in Macedonia.

There were some poor churches in Macedonia. They didn't have much to give, but Paul tells us and the church at Corinth that they gave out of their poverty. They joyfully gave out of their poorness. It's almost like an oxymoron that you can give joyfully out of poorness. They gave abundantly out of nothing. Paul says they gave even of themselves. In fact, Paul says, "they begged us to allow them to share in the ministry of the saints."

Notice that verse 8 says, "I speak not by commandment." In other words, I'm not talking about the tithe. I speak not about the law, but I'm talking about giving because God has been so good. The poor Macedonian churches gave, and they gave of themselves. They begged to be able to share. They felt that because they had been so blessed, they just had to give.

Paul also says that they gave out of sincerity of their love to prove the sincerity of their love. In other words, if we really love Jesus, we can prove the sincerity of our love by giving generously to the work of the Lord. Likewise, God says to us that we can prove the sincerity of our love by the giving of ourselves and by supporting the ministry that God has so blessed us with. Paul tells the church, "*I know the ministry here at Corinth; you have a great ministry of utterance. Then he names their ministries and says, 'While you are abounding in all that grace, don't forget also that there is grace in giving'*" (v.7).

> *If we really love Jesus, we can prove the sincerity of our love by giving generously to the work of the Lord.*

Application

We can apply Paul's words to churches today. God is saying to many churches, "I know you have a great Sunday School. I know you have a great music ministry and great worship and a great facility and great discipleship and all of this. But while you abound in all these graces, don't forget the grace of giving."

A Living Example

Paul says these poor Macedonian churches were so faithful in their giving that they could be used as an example of God's goodness and grace. This says to us that the stewardship of Jesus can become complete in us. We could be so good in our giving, proving the sincerity of our love in the grace of giving that we could be used as an example of the stewardship of Jesus Christ.

The poor Macedonian churches were so good in their giving; it prompted Paul to remind the church at Corinth, and us, that we are blessed through His poorness.

For Ye Know (Verse 9)

The word "know" in Greek and Hebrew means more than to understand. Today when we hear the word "know" it means that we understand, but that's not what the Bible is saying. The Bible says the word "know" means that something has taken place intimately. For example, when Mary had a baby and had not known a man. Or

Don't forget the grace of giving.

when in Abraham's old age he knew Sarah. "Know" biblically means to have an intimate relationship.

And so Paul says he's not talking about whether we understand. We've had an intimate relationship with the grace of our Lord Jesus Christ. We've experienced Him. We know Him. We've been there. Nobody has to tell us about it. We didn't get it vicariously. We know. We've entered an intimate relationship. We've experienced the grace. We know what God has done. He's entered intimately into our hearts. By grace we know Him.

Blessings on Top of Blessings

We know grace. "Grace" by definition, both biblically and in Webster's Dictionary, means unmerited favor. We did not deserve to be saved. God has not dealt with us according to what we deserve, but He's dealt with us according to grace. But the word "grace" here implies even more than undeserved favor. It implies that God has laid on us blessings on top of blessings. He didn't just bless us one time but He has been blessing us for a long time.

Some of us experience intimately the grace of a blessing laid upon us. When we couldn't afford something, God gave it to us anyway. We know that kind of grace. Because of His grace, we have been blessed abundantly, over and over again. As a matter of fact, the Lord is blessing us right now.

How Rich?

How rich was Jesus Christ? I could tell you in biblical terms, but let me declare that Jesus Christ is a trillion times richer than Bill Gates ever will be. Microsoft goes up four points, and Bill Gates makes nearly $1 million in one day. But Jesus Christ is a trillion times richer than Bill Gates ever will be.

How rich was Jesus? According to John 1, He possessed the very nature of the fullness of God. According to Jude 1:24–25, He dwelt in the glory of the majesty and the dominion that God had. According to 1 Timothy 6:16, He dwelt in a light that no man could approach in all the splendor and brilliance of the Godhead. According to James 1:17, He possessed every good and perfect thing that could be possessed. According to Revelation 4 and 5, He had all worship and adoration of all heavenly things. Everything in heaven bowed down before Him. Everything! The celestial beings, all the Old Testament characters that He had put in paradise—they all worshiped Him. Abraham, a man of faith, bowed down before Him in heaven. Enoch, who was a friend of God, bowed down in heaven. Ezekiel and Isaiah spent twenty-four hours a day in heaven just bowing down to a holy God, giving Him the highest praise. Twenty-four hours a day the angels gave God highest praise. Jesus received continuous praise twenty-four hours a day, yet He left all of that. He left heaven's throne. He owned everything that could be possessed, but He left it all. For though He was rich, yet He became poor so that ye might be rich.

How Poor?

He became poor. The question might be, "How poor?" Jesus' becoming poor refers to His incarnation. He left all of His glorious riches and became a humble man. The Lord took on flesh and blood. The holy God took the lowliest place. The sovereign Lord became the subject. The beloved became the rejected. The perfect One became the sacrifice for sin. Life became a substitute for death. *"Let this mind be in you, which was also in Christ Jesus: Who, being in the form of God, thought it not robbery to be equal with God: But made himself of no reputation, and took upon him the form of a servant, and was made in the likeness of men: And being found in fashion as a man, he humbled himself, and became obedient unto death, even the death of the cross"* (Philippians 2:5–8 - KJV). He *became* poor. He didn't have to become poor. He volunteered to become poor. He could have stayed on the heavenly throne, but He became poor. He left His riches and throne to be born poor in a manger. He was born from the womb of a poor peasant girl. He was raised in a poor family of a poor carpenter. He lived a life of poorness.

"Foxes have holes, and birds of the air have nests; but the Son of man hath not where to lay His head" (Luke 9:58 - KJV). He died a poor, criminal death and was buried in a borrowed tomb. He was born a poor man, lived as a poor man, and died a poor man.

Although He died poor, He arose rich with all power in His hands. He said those who receive Him can become sons and daughters. Our Father is rich. The earth and the fullness thereof belong to Him. Our Father owns all the cattle on the hills. He's rich in omniscience, omnipotence, and omnipresence. He knows all, has all power, and is everywhere at all times.

We became rich in His poorness, but we remain rich in His richness. We are rich in salvation. We are rich in sanctification. We are rich in justification. We are rich in holiness. We are rich in power. We are rich in love. We are rich in mercy, in peace, in joy. Because He died, He became poor for our sakes and through His poverty we became rich, but He arose and because He arose, we remain rich.

Summary

God admonishes us and the Corinthians to take notice and model the Macedonian church in giving. The Macedonian church was poor, yet gave generously.

Likewise, Christ became poor for our sakes so we might have riches. By knowing the grace of our Lord Jesus Christ we are blessed through His poorness (poverty). Because of our intimate relationship with Christ, we experience (know) His grace, we are blessed abundantly—equivalent to having blessings on top of blessings. God was not just rich, but God was very, very rich. Yet, He became very, very poor that we might have all that He owns. He died in poorness but was raised in glory, and because He arose, not only are we blessed, but we remain blessed.

CHAPTER TWELVE

Blessed Through Fear of the Lord

Psalm 112:1–10 (KJV)

1 *PRAISE ye the Lord. Blessed is the man that feareth the Lord, that delighteth greatly in his commandments.*

2 *His seed shall be mighty upon earth: the generation of the upright shall be blessed.*

3 *Wealth and riches shall be in his house: and his righteousness endureth for ever.*

4 *Unto the upright there ariseth light in the darkness: he is gracious, and full of compassion, and righteous.*

5 *A good man sheweth favour, and lendeth: he will guide his affairs with discretion.*

6 Surely he shall not be moved for ever: the righteous shall be in everlasting remembrance.

7 He shall not be afraid of evil tidings: his heart is fixed, trusting in the LORD.

8 His heart is established, he shall not be afraid, until he see his desire upon his enemies.

9 He hath dispersed, he hath given to the poor; his righteousness endureth for ever; his horn shall be exalted with honour.

10 The wicked shall see it, and be grieved; he shall gnash with his teeth, and melt away: the desire of the wicked shall perish.

From Genesis to Revelation, God continually prevails and repeatedly suggests ways He could bless us. The psalmist tells us in Psalm 112 that we can be blessed through the fear of God. Blessed is the person that feareth the Lord.

> *Those who fear the Lord are among those who experience a right-now blessed life.*

Those who fear the Lord are among those who experience a right-now blessed life. This psalm is not dealing with the blessing in heaven. But those who fear the Lord experience an existential, right-now, blessed life. Those who fear the Lord are among the blessed ones. Also, the fear of God produces a fearless, blessed life. If we fear God, we'll never have to fear man.

156

The Origin of Wisdom

The fear of the Lord is the beginning of wisdom. Wisdom did not begin in kindergarten. Wisdom did not begin with the learning of the "three r's"—reading, (w)riting, and (a)rithmetic. Wisdom did not begin with philosophy. Wisdom did not begin with existentialism. Wisdom did not begin with behavioral science or rationalism or statistical analysis. The fear of the Lord, the Bible teaches, is the beginning of wisdom. So we are commanded to fear God. *"And now, Israel, what doth the Lord thy God require of thee, but to fear the Lord thy God"* (Deuteronomy 10:12 - KJV).

> The fear of the Lord is the beginning of wisdom.

The Biblical Meaning of Fear

What does fear mean? A biblical, working definition is needed. Biblically speaking, fear does not mean the type of fear that first pops into our mind—fear from a ghost or a monster. Fear means to revere God. Our fear grows out of reverence to Him. It means to revere God enough to be scared of His wrath.

The Bible tells us that we should fear God because He can destroy both body and soul. *"And fear not them which kill the body, but are not able to kill the soul: but rather fear him which is able to destroy both soul and body in hell"* (Matthew 10:28 - KJV). We don't have to fear what can destroy only the body. Murderers can only destroy the body. But God can destroy body and soul. The fear of God means to revere Him enough to be scared not to keep His commandments. If we fear Him and reverence His awesome position and power enough, He will put us in the channel of His blessing stream. God's grace is sufficient to cover our sins, but fear of Him will bless us right now.

Fear means to revere God.

Worldly Cockiness

The problem is that too many Christians are just plain cocky. There is a difference between being confident and being cocky. If we are confident, we have our trust in God. There is such a thing as being spiritually confident and that's good. But there is another thing called worldly cockiness. Those who are worldly cocky have egos that are so big they are not scared of man or God.

Those who fall into that type of cockiness will be grieved. They shall be among the ones who will gnash their teeth, and their very desires will perish. *"The wicked shall see it, and be grieved; he shall gnash with his teeth, and melt away: the desire of the wicked shall perish"* (Psalm 112:10 - KJV). According to the psalmist, we are either blessed or cursed. The psalms give two examples, the righteous and the wicked. This means there is no middle ground. We are either blessed or cursed.

Blessings vs. Curses

Some of us are cursed and don't know we're cursed because we don't know what it means to be blessed. We don't know we are cursed because we really don't know what it means to be among the blessed ones. But we are either blessed or cursed; there's no neu-

It means to revere God enough to be scared of His wrath.

tral ground in God's kingdom. We are going either forward or backward.

Which are you? Are you blessed or are you cursed? Which road are you traveling? Are you traveling the blessed road or are you traveling the cursed road? I think we want to travel the blessed road, don't you? So, you must look at what God teaches us about being blessed by fearing the Lord.

An Expository Lesson from a Psalmist

Psalm 112 was written by somebody like you and I that God worked with and dealt with enough to inspire him to say, *"Praise ye the Lord. Blessed is the man that feareth the Lord"* (v.1).

This psalm could be entitled, "The Prosperity of the Righteous" because fear of God ultimately leads to righteousness. Righteousness always stands in the flow of God's blessings. So notice Psalm 112, like 111 and 113, begins by saying "Praise ye the Lord, Hallelujah." Often we read, "Praise ye the Lord," at the end of the Psalm. This psalmist doesn't say "Praise God" at the end; he has experienced something, so he says, "Praise ye the Lord. Blessed is the man who feareth the Lord."

> *Righteousness always stands in the flow of God's blessings.*

If you fear the Lord, your children shall be blessed. If you are blessed, your children will be blessed. For no other reason, they are blessed to have blessed parents. If you are blessed in the community where you live and men find favor with you in the community, your children will find favor in that community. Likewise, your children are blessed in righteousness if they come out of a righteous home. If we have prayer and testimony in the home, the children will be affected by it somewhere down the line. *"Train up a child in the way he should go: and when he is old, he will not depart from it"* (Proverbs 22:6 - KJV).

Train up a child in righteousness, not just going to church. Some of us go to church and have no righteousness in the home. We're just religious folks, and our children know it. If we go to rap sessions in teen conferences, they tell how hypocritical Mama and Daddy really are. "They come every Sunday, Pastor, but when they go home . . ." Our children are smart. They learn from what they see Mama and Daddy do. If we fear (revere) God in our homes, we will be blessed, and our children, our seed will be blessed. God's Word does not lie.

Verse 3 clearly says that a person who has fear of the Lord is blessed materially and/or spiritually. Some people have a problem with material blessings, but the Bible really teaches that we can be blessed materially and/or spiritually.

If we fear the Lord, our children shall be blessed.

The psalmist is saying we will be blessed materially, but if we are not blessed materially we will be blessed spiritually. Either way, we will be blessed. We will be blessed with wealth and riches or we will be blessed spiritually. I like the way the songwriter put it: "Any way you want to do it, Lord, just bless me."

Verse 4 says to the person who feareth the Lord, a light will arise out of his darkness. First, this acknowledges that we are going to have some darkness. It acknowledges that even blessed people have troubled times. We can be among the blessed ones and still have crises and adversity in our lives. So, even though we have some dark times, to those who fear the Lord, light will arise out of the darkness. In other words, for those who fear the Lord, a good thing will come out of a bad thing. Maybe that's why Paul was inspired to write, *"All things work together for good to them that love God, to them who are the called according to his purpose"* (Romans 8:28 - KJV).

> *We can be among the blessed ones and still have a crises or adversity in our lives.*

Verse 5 says that a good man shows favor to others. He lends to folks. When I was growing up, it bothered me that everybody ate at my daddy's house. It bothered me when I was young that when I went to Grandmama's house, she would invite people from church to dinner. They weren't interested in church, they just wanted to come because they knew Grandmama would invite them home for dinner. But her seed was blessed. I'm a part of her seed and my daddy's seed. Their seed was blessed. If you fear the Lord, your children will be blessed.

Verse 6 says the righteous shall be remembered long after they are gone. If you fear the Lord you will be remembered. Verse 7 says that they shall not be afraid of evil tidings. In other words, they are not afraid of what's going to happen in the future. Many people are scared of what's

A good man shows favor to others.

going to happen before it ever happens. We can't do anything because we're afraid it's going to come out badly. Those who fear the Lord don't worry about bad things that will happen in the future.

Verse 9 says those that fear the Lord give to the poor and their horn shall be exalted. The horn is a symbol of power and it's like the horns on a bull or a moose. The power of those who fear will be exalted. They don't have to exalt themselves. They don't have to lift their own power. God will exalt power in them because they fear the Lord.

Summary

God promises in Psalm 112 that those who fear the Lord will be blessed. Fear is defined as revering and honoring God. Because we fear (revere) Him, we keep

His commandments. Revering and honoring Him leads to righteousness, and He explicitly tells us that the righteous shall prosper. The opposite of fear is "worldly cockiness" which leads to devastation. Those who fear the Lord shall be blessed because fear is the beginning of wisdom. Those who fear the Lord may be blessed materially and/or spiritually. Those who fear the Lord shall be blessed in that 1) their children shall be blessed, 2) they will be able to overcome crises, 3) they will be remembered for a long time, 4) they will be given exalted power, and 5) they shall not be afraid or worry about the future.

Those who fear the Lord don't worry about bad things that will happen in the future.

CHAPTER THIRTEEN

Blessed Through Perseverance

Genesis 32:24–29 (KJV)

25 *And Jacob was left alone; and there wrestled a man with him until the breaking of the day.*

25 *And when he saw that he prevailed not against him, he touched the hollow of his thigh; and the hollow of Jacob's thigh was out of joint, as he wrestled with him.*

26 *And he said, Let me go, for the day breaketh. And he said, I will not let thee go, except thou bless me.*

27 *And he said unto him, What is thy name? And he said, Jacob.*

28 *And he said, Thy name shall be called no more Jacob, but Israel: for as a prince hast thou power with God and with men, and hast prevailed.*

29 *And Jacob asked him, and said, Tell me, I pray thee, thy name. And he said, Wherefore is it that thou dost ask after my name? And he blessed him there.*

"And he said, Let me go, for the day breaketh. And he said, I will not let thee go, except thou bless me" (Genesis 32:26). *"I will not,"* Jacob said to God. *"I will not let you go until you bless me."* Perseverance is a key factor to being blessed.

Don't Get Out of Line

Recently, I was in a bank not known for its fast service. I was in a hurry and the line was long. I needed to get back to the church. After looking at my watch several times, I decided I would hold on and stand there for a while. People in line were restless and began to drop out of line. One man became disgusted, dropped out, and left. The next man dropped out. About five people dropped out of line. The next thing I knew, I was first in line.

Stay in the line and we may be next on God's blessing agenda.

We must learn not to get out of line. Saints are dropping out of the blessing line every day. We must stay in the line that we may be next on God's blessing agenda. We must stay in the line; hold on and keep on praying.

An Old Testament Example

Jacob was one who held on until his change came. Jacob told God I will not let you go until you bless me. I can just hear the conversation.

Here is God, and this man is saying, "I won't let you go until you bless me." God said, "What's your name?" He said, "My name is Jacob." God said, "No, your name used to be Jacob, but your change has come. The name Jacob means deceiver, a supplanter, a trickster. No longer is your name Jacob, but your name is Israel, which means prince that now has power with God because thou has prevailed with God and with man." Jacob held on for his blessing. Jacob held on until his change came.

> We need to hold on until our change comes.

We need to hold on until our change comes. We cannot get out of line. We must stay in line and hold fast for there is a light at the end of the tunnel. We must hold fast; there is a blessing on the other side of through. We are blessed through perseverance.

Jacob was one of Isaac's twin boys. One was named Esau and the other was named Jacob. Esau was his dad's favorite because Esau was what dads like in a son. He was a hunter and an athlete. Today, Esau would be playing shortstop, pitcher, catcher, quarterback, and would be the captain of the teams.

But Jacob was a Mama's boy. He hung around the kitchen and cooked biscuits with his mama. He learned to talk and think like his mama.

Jacob was a trickster, and he and his mama contrived a way to trick Esau out of his blessing. Jacob stole two things from Esau: his birthright and his blessing. Jacob was a bad boy and had to get out of town quickly.

Sometimes our change doesn't come until we get tired of running.

In the scripture referenced, approximately twenty years have passed. Jacob has been living the life of a liar and looking over his shoulder because Esau may be coming over the hill at any minute.

Sometimes our change doesn't come until we get tired of running. Jacob was tired of looking over his shoulder. When we get sick and tired of being sick and tired, sometimes our change comes.

Jacob was now willing to give back the material blessings out of which he had tricked Esau. He could not give back the spiritual blessings, but he recanted his position concerning the material blessings. He sent Esau money, gold, cattle, goats and everything. He recanted his position. In essence, he repented. We have to repent if we want our change to come.

God is calling us to get rid of that rebellious spirit, repent, and say, "Lord, I've been wrong." In verse 24, Jacob was left alone. Twenty years have passed since he left his daddy's house, and now Jacob knows Esau's location. He has already sent messengers with gold out to Esau.

A Lesson Learned

If we don't get our blessings God's way, our blessings will haunt us. We may think we are blessed right now but if our blessing is not God-approved, our blessing will haunt us. Father Isaac said to Jacob, "I know you tricked me, but I'm still going to bless you." Isaac could have changed his mind when he found out that Jacob had tricked him, but he blessed him anyway. But it does no good for our earthly daddy to bless us if God doesn't bless us. Our mother might leave us the family house, but we need God's blessing on it. Our daddy may leave us the family estate, but we need God's blessing on it. Our daddy may leave us his Mercedes or his new Town Car in his

> *We may think we are blessed right now but if our blessing is not God-approved, our blessing will haunt us.*

will, but if God hasn't blessed it then it's going to haunt us. We need God's blessings on everything. If our blessings are not God-approved, they will haunt us or we will eventually lose them. *"The blessing of the LORD, it maketh rich, and he addeth no sorrow with it"* (Proverbs 10:22 - KJV).

A Wrestling Match

Jacob was left alone and he wrestled with a man until the break of day. He wrestled with him at night. We don't know whether we're reading about a vision or dream or an actuality, but we do know that it was night and many things happen at night. God works at night. Jacob was prevailing in the wrestling match. Jacob was wrestling with God and for a while seems to have been winning.

In my imagination, I believe Jacob had God in a full Nelson. God didn't hit Jacob. God just touched his thigh. Jacob went, "Oowww." It looks like Jacob was winning the battle, and God just touched his thigh. But even with his thigh out of joint, Jacob was still holding on. He knew for sure by now that his arms were too short to box with God. He knew that the only way, the only reason he was prevailing was by the grace of God. He knew that God had just let him win for a while.

Jacob had come to the point where he realized he couldn't win over God, but he still held on. And Jacob told God, "I'm going to hold on. You've knocked my thigh out of joint. There's no telling what you might do to me next. I know I'm not winning this thing, but I'm going to hold on. My thigh is out. I'm hurting. I have pain shooting up in my cranial nerve. My eyes look like they're going to blink out. I feel like I'm going to have a heart attack, but I'm going to hold on. I'm going to hold on until my change comes."

God looked at Jacob and said, "What's your name?" Jacob answered, "My name is Jacob, which means supplanter. I've been a liar and a trickster all my life." God said, "Your name is no longer Jacob. Your name now is Israel, which means that you have prevailed with God and with man, and I'm going to bless you right here." Jacob named the place Peniel, which means that he had come face to face with God. Jacob left that scene with a limp when the sun came up.

Are we struggling with God? Jacob held on until the sun came out, until the break of day. Break of day may be right around the corner. We must hold on for our blessing. We must hold on through the nighttime. Nighttime may be long. Nighttime may be one big midnight after another. But we must hold on until the sun comes up because scripture declares that *"weeping may endure for a night but joy cometh in the morning"* (Psalm 30:5 - KJV).

Detachment

Why aren't we blessed? The answer is, "Because of detachment." We have a problem with not being attached. We're not holding on because we have cut ourselves off from the blessing. We have cut ourselves off from the blessing giver. If you abide in God. If you'll hold on to God and His Word holds on to you, you can ask what you will and it shall be done unto you (John 15:7).

> We're not holding on because we have cut ourselves off from the blessing.

We think we are attached when we really are not. Some are deceived by a holy self-righteousness and think they are attached, but they are really off the vine. If we want to be blessed, we have to be on the vine. *"I am the true vine, and my Father is the husbandman"* (John 15:1 - KJV). If we're not on the vine, we need to get back on the vine. We must hold on till our blessings come. Winds may blow, but we must stay on the vine. Storms may rise, but we must stay on the vine. Heavy rain may beat down on the vine, but we must stay on the vine until our blessing comes. We must stay on the vine until our change comes.

Being Blessed Requires a Struggle

Not only do we have to persevere, but we have to struggle. In life, anything worth having is worth working for. We shouldn't appreciate anything given to us on a silver platter. That's why God wants us to struggle. If we don't struggle, we will not have any gratitude. If we don't struggle, we will have no thanksgiving. If we have no thanksgiving, we will have no praise. Do we ever wonder why the new generation seems not to

Stay on the vine until our change comes.

have very much gratitude? It's our fault, not theirs. We give them too much. We need to make sure our children work for what they have.

Jacob had to prevail with God and with man. Some of us are very satisfied in our struggle in our relationship with God, but we don't want to struggle in our relationship with other people. Some of us will tithe to God, but disobey God's Word concerning our relationships with other people.

We will disobey Matthew 18:15 that says if we have ought with our brother, we need to go to our brother and confront the fault. We will disobey Matthew 5:23 that says if we bring our gift to the altar and we have ought with our brother, we should leave our gift there

> We must experience some transformation.

and go back and make the situation straight. We disobey these scriptures, which means we are unattached, we are detached. We are not as blessed as God desires because we are not struggling to stay attached to the vine.

Blessings Require Change

We have to persevere in the struggle, and we have to persevere for the change. Jacob persevered till his change came. Jacob's name was changed from Jacob to Israel. The twelve sons of Jacob became the twelve tribes of Israel. Jacob's name, which orginally meant trickster, now means prince that has power, that has prevailed with man and with God. If we want to be blessed, some transformation has to take place in our lives. *"And be not conformed to this world: but be ye transformed by the renewing of your mind, that ye may prove what is that good, and acceptable, and perfect, will of God"* (Romans 12:2 - KJV). We must experience some transformation.

Hold On in Your Brokenness

If we want to be blessed, we have to be broken. After Jacob had struggled with God, the sun rose and he went away limping because his hip was out of joint. We need to understand that Jacob limped for the rest of his life. His limp represented his brokenness. His limp represented the fact that his deceitful, deceiving, evil spirit was broken.

> If we want to be blessed, we have to be broken.

His limp represented that his lying spirit had been broken. Jacob's limp always reminded him of his old self. Any time Jacob's humanity began to rise too much, God would shoot a little pain down in his limp to remind him that his arms were too short to box with God. Jacob was reminded through his limp to stay humble.

Like Jacob, I too have a limp in my life. I am blessed, but I, also like Paul, have a thorn in my flesh. Every time my ego gets inflated, God deflates it with my thorn because He wants to use me and bless me. My limp reminds me of the day that my change came. My limp will remind me that there is a blessing on the other side of through. My limp reminds me that I struggled with Him till I was blessed. My limp will remind me that I always may be next in line. My limp reminds me that we all can be blessed through perseverance, so we should hold on until our blessing comes.

Summary

Perseverance is a key factor in being blessed. The familiar scripture narrative that tells of how Jacob wrestled with God and held on until his blessing came teaches us a valuable lesson on perseverance. We learn: 1) if our blessings are not approved by God, they will later haunt us, 2) we must stay attached to the blessing source, 3) to be blessed we must struggle, 4) to be blessed we must change, and 5) to be blessed we must be broken. We ought, therefore, to remain in the line until our change comes because God blesses through our perseverance.

Blessed Through Right Giving

2 Cor 9:5–11 (KJV)

5 *Therefore I thought it necessary to exhort the brethren, and they would go before unto you, and make up beforehand your bounty, whereof ye had notice before, that the same might be ready, as a matter of bounty, and not as of covetousness.*

6 *But this I say, He which soweth sparingly shall reap also sparingly; and he which soweth bountifully shall reap also bountifully.*

7 *Every man according as he purposeth in his heart, so let him give; not grudgingly, or of necessity: for God loveth a cheerful giver.*

8 *And God is able to make all grace abound toward you; that ye, always having all sufficiency in all things, may abound to every good work:*

9(As it is written, He hath dispersed abroad; he hath given to the poor: his righteousness remaineth for ever.

10 Now he that ministereth seed to the sower both minister bread for your food, and multiply your seed sown, and increase the fruits of your righteousness;)

11 Being enriched in every thing to all bountifulness, which causeth through us thanksgiving to God.

This New Testament scripture is one of the most critical scriptures anywhere in the Bible. It teaches us about Christian giving. In these verses we can see what God has to say about Christian giving as it applies to His Word and promises. We can be blessed through right or correct giving.

God has enabled us to grow our own blessings through right giving.

God has enabled us to grow our own blessings through right giving. God has enabled us to plant a garden of blessings. We know about farming chickens; we can also farm blessings. We know about having a garden of tomatoes; we can also have a garden full of blessings.

A Garden of Blessings

An analogy can be drawn of a garden. If we plant a tomato seed, we don't get just one tomato; a stalk comes up and there are many tomatoes on it. When we plant a corn seed, we don't get just one ear of corn, a corn stalk comes up and bears many ears of corn. Many apples come from one apple seed.

We don't plant a blessing seed and get one blessing; we plant a blessing seed and get many blessings. The blessing seeds we plant today will bless us in the future. God's return will always be greater than our service rendered. Serving God is a good investment. That is why the songwriter wrote, "It pays to serve Jesus. It pays every day. It pays to serve Jesus every step of the way."

Sowing and Reaping

There is a relationship between sowing and reaping. There is a relationship between planting and harvesting. This is a natural law, but the natural law also applies to a spiritual law. Those who sow sparingly, reap sparingly. Those who sow bountifully shall reap bountifully. That is God's law. God put it in nature and He put it in spirit.

> *God's return will always be greater than our service rendered.*

I am often asked, "Should I tithe from my gross or my net?" The real answer to that is, "How do we want to be blessed? Netly or grossly?" The real answer comes from a natural law. If we sow sparingly, we will reap sparingly. If we sow bountifully, we will reap bountifully.

A Purposed Heart and a Willing Heart

The writer of the referenced scripture, Paul, goes on to teach us how to give correctly in order to be blessed correctly: "Let every man purpose it in his heart." In other words, God is saying to the leaders of the Church, don't stay in church all day begging for money. Purpose your giving in your heart before you go to church. Pray about it. God says that we need to have already thought about what we will give before we get to church. We need to be prepared for it. So when we get to church, we need to just worship. We don't need to spend time talking about the collection. Every Sunday should not be spent talking about needing more money. The preacher needs to divide rightly the Word of God with the collection already taken. Paul said that every man should purpose in his heart, not grudgingly, but willingly. In other words, our hearts should lead our hands.

> *Purpose your giving in your heart before you go to church.*

Ye Know

In a previous chapter, I talked about the meaning of the word "know" and how in 2 Corinthians 8:9 does not mean to understand, but in biblical language, is an intimate term. I talked about how it confers and denotes intimacy, like with Mary who had a baby and had not known a man or, like Abraham knew Sarah. I also went on to talk about the fact that this verse implies that by grace we know the Lord; we've experienced the Lord; we know what He's done. I thought it was worth repeating, to say this, I don't have to tell you about Him. We have an intimate relationship with the graces of God. Ye know. We may act like we don't know. We may hold our hands tight;

> Why does God love a cheerful giver? Because He sees His own character in a cheerful giver.

hold on to our pocketbooks and not give, but it is not because we don't know. Ye know. God has entered into our lives. We have been intimate with Him. Ye know the grace of our Lord Jesus Christ. We know that for our sakes, though He was rich, He thought it not robbery to become poor so that through His poorness, through His poverty, we might be rich. Because we know God, we ought to give right and be blessed.

A Cheerful Heart

Not only to give it in our heart, but give it cheerfully. "Cheerfully" in Greek means hilariously. God loves a cheerful giver. Why does God love a cheerful giver? Because He sees His own character in a cheerful giver. The nature of God's character is cheerful. God himself is a cheerful giver. So a cheerful giver is like Jesus. Maybe some of us need to stop being hypocritical, and stop singing, "I want to be more and more like Jesus." We can't be like Jesus until we become cheerful givers.

Cheerful giving waters and fertilizes the seeds that we plant in our blessing garden. If we sow our garden bountifully and purposely with a willing heart, then the water and the fertilizer will come from our cheerfulness. Cheerfulness will cultivate our garden.

God's Promise

In addition, God gives a promise in 2 Corinthians 9:8 (KJV) that *"he is able to make all graces abound toward you; that ye, always having all sufficiency in all things, may abound to every good work."* God promises that if we give right, we will not lack for anything His grace can provide. For example, when I testify to what my wife and I are contributing to a capital fund campaign, some might wonder how we are able to do it. First, God promises. God promises that I will not lack for anything when I give rightly. This is a promise from God. God also promises that I cannot get hurt by right giving. God promises that none will suffer loss through right giving. We cannot give right and then go without. God is able. God will provide the right giver with everything he or she needs. We know this. We may not want to hear it, but we know it.

Covetousness

What, then, is our problem? We may have a problem with covetousness. Verse 5 says to give as a matter of bounty, not a matter of covetousness. Covetousness means to have more than enough and to desire more—greed. Greedy for money. Covetousness is that extreme consideration for self

> *God promises that if we give right, we will not lack for anything His grace can provide.*

that makes it possible not only to neglect the needs of others, but also to hurt others to secure selfish desires. One of the Ten Commandments is, *"Thou shalt not covet thy neighbour's house, thou shalt not covet thy neighbour's wife, nor his manservant, nor his maidservant, nor his ox, nor his ass, nor any thing that is thy neighbour's"* (Exodus 20:17 - KJV).

> Covetousness is that extreme consideration for self that makes it possible not only to neglect the needs of others, but also to hurt others to secure selfish desires.

Covetousness is dangerous. Covetousness has been labeled as the preeminent idolatry. Covetousness is a root sin, which means that all other sins grow out of covetousness. Covetousness is a consuming cancer. Once covetousness sets in, it metastasises and begins to spread like a cancer. Covetousness is like a fatal drug. It is impossible for us to be of Christian character when we have a spirit of covetousness.

Right Giving

Right giving is the best cure for covetousness. Right giving is the best medicine for covetousness. Right giving is the best antidote for a bad case of the disease called covetousness. Right giving is the best prevention for covetousness. Right giving is our best protection against covetousness. Right giving is our best shield, best vaccine, or best inoculation against covetousness.

Preparing recently to go to Africa, I had to be inoculated. I thought I was going to get just one shot.

Ultimately, I had to get about six shots because I needed some booster shots. Some of us need a booster shot for right giving. I am glad that God provides me opportunities to get booster shots against covetousness. We cannot be blessed fully as long as we have a speck of covetousness in us. If we have any covetousness in us, the only way we can get rid of it is to give right.

God gives us what we have so He can give us more. In other words, God gave us what we have and He wants to give us more. Verse 10 says that He who supplies the seed to the sower will supply and multiply our seed for sowing and increase the harvest of our righteousness. God gave us the seed. God gave us the first apple seed, the first tomato seed, the first blessing, the first piece of money. The only reason He gave us the piece of money we have is so that He can give us more money. He wants to bless us. The question is how does our garden grow?

> It is impossible for us to be of Christian character when we have a spirit of covetousness.

Right Giving Is Liberating

Liberal giving liberates us, sets us free. We must be free to be blessed. We have our blessing (seed) wrapped up in our own self, and we have to release it. Think about it. Having our blessing in us. And as long as it remains in us, in our own hands, God cannot bless us. Somehow we have to sow our seed. We have to release it.

Right Giving Gives God Glory

Right giving gives glory to the unspeakable gift with thanksgiving and praise. *"Those you help will be glad not only because of your generous gifts to themselves and to others, but they will praise God for this proof that your deeds are as good as your doctrine"* (2 Cor 9:13 - TLB). In other words, they will praise God that we are not just talking the talk, but we are walking the walk. Thanks be to God for the unspeakable gift.

> We have our blessing (seed) wrapped up in our own self, and we have to release it

Right Giving Brings Praise

We cannot give right without giving God praise. If we give right, thanksgiving will break out in our hearts. If we give right, something will break out deep down in our souls and be loosed. If we give right, church will break out in our hearts. We cannot give right without having thought about the goodness of Jesus. That is why songwriters penned, "When I think about the goodness of Jesus, and all He's done for me; My very soul cries out Hallelujah! I thank God for saving me," and "When I look back over my life, I can truly say that I've been blessed. I am a testimony."

We need to be set free to cultivate a garden of blessings. We have blessings in our hands, our feet, our mouth, and our lips. We have blessings in our service, our spirit and our gifts. We have blessings in our lives. God wants to bless us and others through our giving.

Summary

God has enabled us to grow our own blessings through right giving. An analogy is drawn from a garden. When we plant a tomato or corn seed, we don't get one tomato or one ear of corn. We get a stalk of tomatoes and corn.

> We need to be set free to cultivate a garden of blessings.

Likewise, we don't plant a blessing seed and get one blessing. Rather, we get many blessings. The blessing seed we plant today will bless us abundantly in the future. There is a spiritual law that applies to sowing and reaping. If we sow a small amount, we will reap a small amount. And if we sow a large amount, we will reap a large amount. We must give right to be blessed right. Right giving involves giving with a willing heart, a purposeful heart, and a cheerful heart. God has promised that if we give right, because of His "able-ness" and grace, we will lack for nothing.

Our problem, however, is covetousness. Covetous-ness is extremely dangerous and can be labeled as pre-eminent idolatry and the root of all sin. Right giving is the best solution for covetousness. Right giving over-comes covetousness by setting us free to give and be blessed. Right giving always results in thanksgiving and praise, thereby giving glory to God. Indeed, God wants to bless us through our giving.

CHAPTER FIFTEEN

Blessed Through the Word of God

Psalm 119:1–2 (KJV)

¹ Blessed are the undefiled in the way, who walk in the law of the LORD.
² Blessed are they that keep his testimonies, and that seek him with the whole heart.

If there is anything that God wants to do, it is to bless us. He wants us joyful, blessed, happy and glad, not depressed, oppressed, suppressed, mad or sad. Psalm 119 is the longest Psalm. It has one hundred and seventy six verses. But the Psalmist sets out by writing a marvelous introductory paragraph in the first two verses, particularly the first seventeen verses as he speaks to us about how we are to be blessed. The one hundred and seventy six verses have one theme and that is the Word of God. He refers to the Word of God in several different terms. He doesn't always use the term *Word*. Sometimes he uses the word *law*. At other times he uses the words *commandments, testimony, precepts, statutes, judgment* or *the way*. So what we are saying is that we are blessed by the law. We are blessed by the commandments. We are blessed by the testimony. We are blessed by the precepts. We are blessed by His statutes, blessed by His judgments, and blessed by the way. We are blessed in that we can be blessed through the Word of God. Every verse in this long 119th Psalm deals in some way with the Word of God. Sometimes the Psalmist is speaking of a praise for God's Word. At other times he is expressing love for God's Word. And at other times he is just praying for grace to conform to God's Word. He says that God's Word tastes good to him, and he loves the Word of God. He thanks God for the Word. And he often just says, I need help Lord, by your grace to be able to conform to your Word.

I am proposing that blessed are those who hear, read and understand His Word, and also keep His Word. I believe that more blessed are those who walk, keep and seek His Word. Perhaps "exceedingly blessed" would be the more proper interpretation. Listen to what he says, "Blessed are the undefiled in the way [word], who walk in the law [word] of the LORD. Blessed are they that keep his testimonies [word], and that seek him [His word] with their whole heart."

We are more blessed by walking, keeping, and seeking His word.

We are more blessed by walking, keeping, and seeking His word.

A Testimony from the Psalmist

The author of this great 119th Psalm is unquestionably David. All scholars agree that the literary style and the expressions match David's. Remember, David was a man honored by God. God expressed His honor of David when He said in Acts 13:22 that David was "a man after mine own heart." What an honor. David was inspired to write the 119th Psalm after many trials, tribulations and afflictions. Allow me to fast-forward to verse 71 where David said, "It is good for me that I have been afflicted." You know, it is good to get caught sometimes. I often think about President Bill Clinton and when he was going through his scandal involving his extramarital affairs. How many in the church were sitting in judgment of Bill Clinton? I used to think to myself, "Old Bill got caught. What a blessing he got caught. Some folks in church haven't got caught and are living unrepented lives. Old Bill got a chance to repent. Old Bill may be going to heaven. And folks sitting up in church may be going to hell." It is a blessing to get caught sometimes.

God will usually ring our bells before we get caught. Somebody needs to know that God is ringing their bell right now. He is saying, "Don't let me have to catch you." David said that it was good that he was afflicted. But then he goes on to say that I thank you for your word that taught me. I learned from your word. I was convicted by your word. We need to remember David. He holds the title of being the greatest sinner and the greatest saint of the Old Testament. David was a shepherd who played his harp. David was the hunter and also the hunted, by his father-in-law, King Saul, in the wilderness. Great King David was the conqueror of a great nation. David was an adulterer and a murderer, but David repented and was forgiven. David now directs God's angelic choir. God had David to write these words to us: "Blessed are the undefiled in the way, who

It is a blessing to get caught sometimes.

walk in the law of the Lord. Blessed are they that keep His testimonies and seek Him with their whole heart."

Triply Blessed

Here is what God is saying to us. God is saying that we are triply blessed. How? We are blessed if we walk in the Word. We are blessed when we keep the Word. We are blessed when we seek the Word.

First, blessed are those who walk in the Word. To walk in the Word means to live happily by the rules of God. To those who walk in the Word, religion is not something out of the way. To those who walk in the Word of God, religion is the main road and the only road. This holy walk is not so much a work in progress

To walk in the word means to live happily by the rules of God.

as it is a walk in progress. Those who walk in His Word are never idle. They never lie down. They never loaf. They continually walk onward toward their desired aim which is holiness. Those who walk in the Word are guaranteed to be blessed. Why? Those who walk in God's Word walk in God's company. They have God's smile; they have God's joy; they have God's strength; they have God's power. They can't be anything but blessed. They are walking in His Word like

Enoch walked with God. They are walking in His company. They are walking with His strength. They are walking in His joy. They are walking in His smile. They are walking in His power. Psalm 119:105 says, *"Thy word is a lamp unto my feet, and a light unto my path."* I admonish you, if we want to be exceedingly blessed, we need to walk in His Word.

Second, we are to keep His Word. We are blessed by keeping His Word. This is a blessing on top of the first blessing. We are blessed by walking in the Word. But we are even more blessed by keeping His Word. Keeping His Word means that we store up His Word. Those that keep His Word have found His Word and now treasure it. In order to keep His Word, we have to have a firm grip on His Word. In order to have a firm grip on His Word, we must embrace His Word with affection, adoration and love as we would a precious diamond or jewel that we put in a treasury box. But we put His Word in the treasury box of our hearts, much like they kept the Word in the Ark of the Covenant. In the Old Testament the Word or the law, was so precious that it was always kept in the Ark of the Covenant. In the New Testament, we keep it in our hearts. We are to store it up in our hearts. David said in verse 11, *"Thy*

> *Keeping His word means that we store up His word.*

word have I hid in mine heart, that I might not sin against thee." Those who keep God's Word surely must walk in God's Word as well as keep God's Word and be blessed.

Third, not only are we to walk in His Word and keep His Word, but we are also to seek His Word. Those who seek His Word seek God Himself. Seeking God's Word means acting on a desire to commune with Him more closely. It means to enter into a more perfect communion with Him. To seek His Word means to seek His presence. This is what *worship* means. Many of us think *worship* is a noun, instead of a verb. Those who seek His Word try to come into His presence with their whole heart. They seek His face. Interestingly, a blessed person has already found God, yet continues to seek after Him. This sounds like a contradiction, but it is not—those that have found Him, sought Him. I like to call it a holy paradox.

> *Seeking God's word means a desire to commune with Him more closely.*

Now we have a threefold blessing. We are exceedingly blessed. We are blessed by walking after Him. We are blessed by storing up the Word of God. And we are blessed by seeking Him. If you are blessed by the Word of God, that means you are blessed triply.

A Divided, But Not Broken Heart vs. A Whole, But Broken Heart

What, then, is our problem. The text speaks to our problem. The text tells us that we don't have a whole heart, that we don't walk, keep and seek Him with a whole heart. Our problem is one of a divided heart, but not yet broken heart. This again seems contradictory—divided but not broken. Here comes another holy paradox. Divided in the sense that we do not wholeheartedly walk, keep and seek His word. Unbroken in the sense that we have not yet been broken. Broken from our fleshly spirit. Broken from loving ourselves and other things more than we love God. To be blessed by God's Word by walking, keeping, and seeking, our heart must be one. Our heart must be made whole. We must walk, keep and seek Him wholeheartedly. For sure we cannot be blessed by His Word by trying to figure Him out mentally. For sure we are not blessed through the cold research methods of the brain. This is not a cerebral thing. This is a heart thing. We don't seek Him to be exceedingly blessed through mental gymnastics. This is a whole heart thing. This is a contrite heart that has been broken

> *We don't walk, keep and seek Him with a whole heart.*

and put back together by the power of God. What a holy paradox. An undivided and unbroken heart may not be blessed. But a broken whole heart will be blessed.

David had his heart broken by the Word of God. David had his heart broken by the prophet Nathan when he told David the story of the little ewe lamb. David the murderer and adulterer was approached by God's man, the prophet Nathan, who told him a simple story. He told David that there was a man who had one little ewe lamb. This lamb was just like a family member. This lamb slept in the bedroom with him. This little lamb ate at the table with him. He loved this little lamb. He was precious. Then there was a man who had a large flock of lambs. He had an abundance of lambs. A visitor came to town, and the man who had a large flock of lambs went and took the man's

We are not blessed through the cold research methods of the brain.

single ewe lamb and slew it to give to the visitor. David was outraged. He asked, "Where is the man?" The scripture says that David pulled his sword and said, "Show him to me." The prophet Nathan said to David, "Thou art the man." David's heart was broken, but he was made whole in his brokenness (2 Samuel 11–12:25 - KJV).

Somebody needs to have a broken heart today in order to serve the Lord. God has the power by the Lamb of God, who was broken and died for us, that our hearts could be broken and made whole to serve Him wholeheartedly. David had sinned against God and man, but he is now the man whom God says is a man after My own heart. If we are to be blessed by His Word we need a whole heart. David said again, *"Create in me a clean heart, O God; and renew a right spirit within me"* (Psalm 51:10 - KJV).

Kept from Defilement

Those who walk, keep, and seek His Word are blessed because they are kept from defilement. Verse 1 says, *"Blessed are the undefiled in the way, who walk in the law of the LORD."* We are blessed if we walk, keep, and seek because we are blessed from being defiled. We can't walk, keep, and seek His word and continue to willfully sin. Forget the word *defilement* for a moment. We cannot walk in His Word, keep His Word, seek His Word, hide His Word, store it up in our hearts, and keep on sinning. We cannot love His Word, study His Word, keep His Word, and willfully do the sinful things we are doing. The Word will either drive us or draw us. That is why so many folks leave the church. They claim they are mad at me or somebody. They are not mad. They just don't want to give up their pleasure. The Word is beginning to clean them. They will either have to leave it alone or clean up. If the Word is preached and taught uncompromisingly, one of two things will happen. We will have to leave the Word alone—walk away from it, or we will have to walk away from that defilement and that sin and that stuff we are doing that we know is not pleasing to God. If we walk, keep, and seek His Word we will be holy. God guarantees it. If we keep, store it up, and hide the Word in our hearts so we won't sin, walk in the way, and seek His presence day by day, we will be holy. Our problem is that we would rather be happy than holy. Our aim should be holiness, but rather our aim is happiness. We want to be happy. We have our rifles out, and we have a scope on it at happiness. Boom! We're shooting at happiness. We are aiming at the wrong thing. We need to aim at holiness. Boom! Holy. Boom! Holy. We need to stop aiming at happiness and start aiming at holiness. The good news is that God has promised that if we hit holiness we will be happy. If we hit holiness, we will be blessed. For blessed are the undefiled who walk in and keep the Word of God.

Rescued But Not Enriched

We can be saved and delivered from some stuff and still not find favor with God and man. God not only wants to save us, but He also wants to enrich our lives. God wants to bless us exceedingly. He wants to bless us. He wants to bless us abundantly. He wants to bless us triply. He wants to bless us quadruply. The believer, the saint who has erred is still saved, but has lost the joy of his salvation. Well, if we have lost it then where do we find it? We find it where we lost it. We lost it in unholiness and we will find it in holiness. We lost it when we fell into sin. We lost it when we backslid. We were saved, and we are saved, but we don't have that joy. We know we don't have it because we can hardly give God praise. Something is holding us back. We have been rescued but we have not yet been enriched. We know we're not walking, keeping and seeking, so we really can't praise God like we want to praise Him because we have hypocritical feelings in us. But if we are walking, and if we are seeking, and if we are keeping, we can give God some praise. We can give Him some worship because we seek His face. We try to come into His presence. Blessed are those that walk in His Word for they are holy, they will be enriched. They walk, they seek, and they keep. They are not only rescued, but they are fortified and enriched.

The Living Word

We are blessed because of His Word and because the Word became flesh, and we beheld His glory full of grace and full of truth. We should be glad that the Word became flesh and brought a little grace into our lives. Aren't we glad that the Word became flesh? In the beginning was the Word, and the Word was God, and the Word was with God, and the Word became flesh and we beheld His glory, full of grace and full of truth. I'm glad about it. We not only have a written word, but also we have a living Word. And because He lives, we can face tomorrow. Because He lives, all fear is gone. We don't just have a written word, but we have a living Word. We can keep the written word, but we can also seek the living Word. We are blessed not only with the written word, but also we are blessed with the living Word. The Bible tells us that in the fullness of time the Word stepped out of eternity. The Word was born in a manger. The Word walked the dusty roads of Palestine—made the lame to walk and the blind to see. The Word ministered to the downtrodden and the brokenhearted. The Word went to Calvary. The Word was rejected by the world. The Word was denied by his family. The Word was condemned by the government. The Word was crucified by Pontius Pilate. The Word hung, bled and died. Do we know who the Word is? The Word is Jesus. Jesus is the living Word. He died. He arose. And He lives.

Summary

We are indeed blessed through the Word of God. David, the psalmist and author of the 119th Psalm, gives us a personal testimony on how we are triply blessed through the Word of God. We are blessed by walking, keeping, and seeking His Word. Walking in His Word means to live happily by the commandments, statutes, and precepts of God. Keeping His Word means to store up His Word in our hearts. Seeking His Word means to desire to commune closely with Him. Our problem is that our hearts are divided but not broken. God desires to bless a broken heart that has been made whole. Those who walk, seek, and keep God's Word are kept from defilement and enriched! Last and most important, we are blessed by the Living Word of God. Jesus is the Living Word!

CHAPTER SIXTEEN

Blessed Through Being Dressed Right

Isaiah 43:18–21 (KJV)

18 *Remember ye not the former things, neither consider the things of old.*

19 *Behold, I will do a new thing; now it shall spring forth; shall ye not know it? I will even make a way in the wilderness, and rivers in the desert.*

20 *The beast of the field shall honour me, the dragons and the owls: because I give waters in the wilderness, and rivers in the desert, to give drink to my people, my chosen.*

21 *This people have I formed for myself; they shall shew forth my praise.*

Mark 2:21–22 (NIV)

21 No one sews a patch of unshrunk cloth on an old garment. If he does, the new piece will pull away from the old, making the tear worse.
22 And no one pours new wine into old wineskins. If he does, the wine will burst the skins, and both the wine and the wineskins will be ruined. No, he pours new wine into new wineskins.

I propose that we have to be dressed right to be blessed right. And, that God is ready to do a new thing in our lives.

Old Testament

The Old Testament text setting is Babylon where God is preparing to release His people from captivity. In the book of Isaish, He's preparing to deliver them one more time. They had already experienced a deliverance from the bondage of Egypt.

We have to be dressed right to be blessed right.

They have been delivered from captivity in Egypt but now He's getting ready to deliver them from Babylon.

From Egypt, God had delivered them out of the hands of Pharaoh and brought them across the Red

Sea. Under Joshua's ministry, God has led them across the Jordan River and has allowed them to defeat the Canaanites. They had conquered Jericho and Ai and even gone against the big giants of the Promised Land. But they messed up in the Promised Land. They had begun to worship heathen traditions. They set idol gods before Jehovah: gods of animals and snakes. They were doing everything against the law of God, even in the Promised Land.

Contemporary Setting

It's hard to believe that someone would do wrong in the Promised Land, isn't it? Well, not really, because we, too, have gone astray in the Promised Land. God has been good to us. God has brought us across our Red Seas and Jordan Rivers, but we have misbehaved in the Promised Land. God has brought us out of slavery in America, yet we messed up in the Promised Land. God has brought us out of the poverty of the rural land, yet we have blundered in the Promised Land. God has brought us out of the poverty of the ghettos of urban cities, but we have made mistakes in the Promised Land. We have moved from being uneducated to having educations, yet we have still messed up.

But the good news is that God is still in the deliverance business. God is still a doctor in the delivery room, and we need some deliverance.

We only have to be saved once, but we can get delivered from a whole lot of things. In our Old Testament text, God was ready to give, impart a new deliverance. God is ready today to grant a new deliverance in our lives. God said *"Behold, I will do a new thing; now it shall spring forth; shall ye not know it?"* (Isaiah 43:19 - KJV).

Know Your Deliverance Need

Do we know what we need deliverance from? God says we really know. We may need deliverance from materialism. We may need deliverance from greediness. We may need deliverance from stinginess. God says, "Shall you not know it? (Isaiah 43:19).

> We only have to be saved once, but we can get delivered from a whole lot of things.

We may need deliverance from an argumentative spirit. It is interesting when you meet somebody with an argumentative spirit. Whatever you say, they will have an argument for it.

We may need deliverance from a holier-than-thou spirit. We may need deliverance from a self-righteous spirit. We may need deliverance from the dangerous spirit of pride. We may need deliverance from a spirit of addiction. We may need deliverance from a spirit of low self-esteem. We may need deliverance from a gossiping spirit. We may need deliverance from a criticizing spirit. We may need deliverance from a complaining spirit.

Notice that we are dealing with a spirit, not an attitude. If it was an attitude, we could get help from a psychologist, psychiatrist, or therapist. But we can't take a spirit to a secular, medical doctor. We have to overcome a spirit with a more powerful spirit. There's only one spirit more powerful than the spirit of the devil, and that's the Holy Ghost spirit of God.

We cannot be delivered while we are still wearing the old self.

Dressed to Be Blessed

One thing is certain, we cannot be blessed right until we are dressed right. To be dressed right we have to pull off the old and put on the new. We cannot be delivered while we are still wearing the old self. God wants to do a new thing in our lives, but we need deliverance from the old. We need deliverance from the past. We need deliverance from the former things. We need deliverance from past hurts. We need deliverance from shame. We need deliverance from old behavior, and we need deliverance from old thinking. We need to be dressed in the new so we can be blessed in the new. Change is necessary for spiritual growth. We won't grow unless we're willing to change.

A New Testament Lesson

Jesus says that no man sews a patch of unshrunk cloth on an old garment. If he does, the new piece will be pulled away from the old, making the tear even worse. We can't even put a new patch on an old suit. Jesus also says, no one pours new wine in an old skin. If he does, both the skin and the wine will be ruined. If we put some new wine in some old wineskins, the fermentation of the new will bubble and the old wineskin will tear apart. All of the wine will run out on the ground and be wasted.

> *We need to be dressed in the new so we can be blessed in the new.*

A New Thing

It's the same when God gets ready to do a new thing—He starts a fermentation in our lives. Something starts bubbling up and the Holy Ghost begins working in our lives. If we do not have a new skin, the old one cannot hold that bubbling. That bubbling will go to waste and all that is new that God wants to bless us with will fall to the ground and be wasted. If we want to have a new thing, we need a new garment, we need new skin. We have to be dressed right to be blessed right.

Dress for Responsibility

First, we have to be dressed right in responsibility. If we are not dressed for the responsibility, that which is new will spill and our blessings will go down the drain.

Dress for Purpose

We have to be dressed right in His purpose. What is His purpose? There are five: worship, fellowship, discipleship, evangelism and ministry. If we are not fulfilling all five of these purposes, we are not dressed right and our blessings will go. We can be spiritual and not be spiritually mature. We are not spiritually mature until we are fulfilling the purposes of God. If we want to be

> *If we want to have a new thing, we need a new garment, we need new skin.*

blessed by God, we need to be spiritually mature. Some of us want to jump and shout but don't want to do anything else; and we call that spiritual. Unless we're fulfilling the fivefold purpose of the church, we are not dressed right in His purpose.

Dress in Aspiration

We need to be dressed right in aspiration. We need to want a blessing. God said in 1 Kings 8:17–19 (KJV), *"And it was in the heart of David my father to build an house for the name of the* Lord *God of Israel. And the* Lord *said unto David my father, "Whereas it was in thine heart to build an house unto my name, thou didst well that it was in thine heart. Nevertheless thou shalt not build the house; but thy son that shall come forth out of thy loins, he shall build the house unto my name."* David wanted to build the house. He had the aspiration to build the house, but he didn't build it. However, because he had aspired to build the house, his son could fulfill the purpose. Some of us don't have the desire. Often we are not blessed because we lack the desire to be blessed. To be really blessed we must aspire to be blessed. God has promised us that He will give us the desire of our hearts. We

> We need to be dressed right in aspiration.

must dress our heart with aspired clothing and be blessed. Personally, I desire every blessing God has for me. No matter how many, if the blessing has my name on it, my desire is to receive it.

Dressed Right in Relationships

We must be dressed right in our relationships, not only with God, but with man. Many of us still think we can have a right relationship with God and not be in right relationship with man. Too often we build our relationships on how others treat us rather than on how God treats us. We seem to think we should treat others as they treat us. No, we should treat others as God treats us. Do we want God to treat us according to what we deserve? God doesn't treat us according to what we deserve; why should we treat others according to what they deserve? Whatever they did to us, God said to treat them as He treats us. If we want to be blessed, we must pull off wrong relationships and put on the garment of right relationships.

Dress Only in New Things

We have to be dressed right in new things and not former things. We can't even consider the former things. The devil wants us to remember all the sins we have committed; he wants us to remember and feel guilty. But God says to consider not the former things. In fact, He says, *"Therefore if any man be in Christ, he is a new creature: old things are passed away"* (2 Corinthians 5:17 - KJV).

> The devil wishes for us to remember all the sins that we have committed. But God says to consider not the former things.

The shame is gone. The hurt is gone. The sin is gone. He has cast it into the sea of forgetfulness, never to be remembered. We have to tell ourselves, "I'm not going to talk about it anymore. I'm not going to rehearse it. I'm not going to believe it." God wants to bring a new thing into my life.

God is able to present us faultless before the throne of grace with exceeding great joy. Because He is able, we can be able. If any man is in Christ, he is a new creature. Further, He said it will not end here because if we can be new down here, He'll make us new up there. The apostle John said in Revelation 21:1–5a (KJV): *"And I saw a new heaven and a new earth: for the first heaven and the first earth were passed away; and there was no more sea. And I John saw the holy city, new Jerusalem, coming down from God out of heaven, prepared as a bride adorned for her husband. And I heard a great voice out of heaven saying, Behold, the tabernacle of God is with men, and he will dwell with them, and they shall be his people, and God Himself shall be with them, and be their God. And God shall wipe away all tears from their eyes; and there shall be no more death, neither sorrow, nor crying, neither shall there be any more pain: for the former things are passed away. And he that sat upon the throne said, Behold, I make all things new."*

Summary

God has a new thing for us. Like He did a new thing when He delivered His people from Babylon, He will do for us now. There is a fresh deliverance awaiting us. But God wants us to be dressed right. God wants us to realize and know for what things we need to be delivered. Knowing what we need to be delivered from helps us dress right for the blessing. Without question, if we want to be blessed we must 1) dress right for responsibility, 2) be dressed in His purpose, 3) be dressed right with aspiration, and 4) be dressed right in our relationships. We must pull off the old skin and put on the new and prepare to receive our blessing.

> *God is able to present us faultless before the throne of grace with exceeding great joy.*

CHAPTER SEVENTEEN

Blessed Through a Portrait of a Blessed Man

Psalm 1:1–6 (KJV)

1 Blessed is the man that walketh not in the counsel of the ungodly, nor standeth in the way of sinners, nor sitteth in the seat of the scornful.

2 But his delight is in the law of the LORD; and in his law doth he meditate day and night.

3 And he shall be like a tree planted by the rivers of water, that bringeth forth his fruit in his season; his leaf also shall not wither; and whatsoever he doeth shall prosper.

4 The ungodly are not so: but are like the chaff which the wind driveth away.

5 Therefore the ungodly shall not stand in the judgment, nor sinners in the congregation of the righteous.

6 For the Lord knoweth the way of the righteous: but the way of the ungodly shall perish.

What does a blessed man look like? What does a blessed woman look like? Can we recognize a blessed person when we see one? Would we know if we were in the company of a blessed person? Do we know if we are blessed? We don't really know a person until we find out what that person is like.

That's why God gives us so many parables describing Himself when He says what the kingdom of heaven is like. Matthew 25:14 (KJV) says, *"For the kingdom of heaven is as a man travelling into a far country, who called his own servants, and delivered unto them his goods."* Luke 15:4–6 says, *"The kingdom of heaven is like a shepherd that leaves the ninety-nine and goes to look for the one that is lost."* Luke 15:8–9 says, *"The kingdom of heaven is like a woman who has ten coins and loses one then searches the house diligently for it."* Luke 15:10–32 says, *"The kingdom of heaven is like a father with two sons, one a prodigal and one an elder son."*

> We cannot really be blessed until we know what a blessed person is like.

God wants us to know what a blessed person is like and so God, through the psalmist, paints a picture of a blessed man. We cannot really be blessed until we know what a blessed person is like. We need a model of whatever we're striving to be. If we are trying to be a basketball player, we need a Michael Jordan for our model. The word "blessed" here means to be happy. Without question, God is saying "happy is the man." So, a blessed person looks happy.

A Picture from Which to Choose

The psalmist paints a picture of a double image. The psalmist seems to be gifted with trick photography, modern split image technology because he puts two pictures on the screen: one of a blessed man and one of a man that is not blessed; one of a happy man and one of an unhappy man; one of a good man and one of a wicked man. The good man is blessed, but the ungodly is not. The ungodly are like chaff driven away by the wind. Therefore, the ungodly shall not stand in the judgment nor sinners in the congregation of the righteous. For the Lord knows the way of the righteous, but the way of the ungodly shall perish. The righteous shall prosper, but the unrighteous shall perish. The choice is ours. Many of us are not blessed because we're walking on the wrong side of the road. We took the wrong exit off life's highway. The blessing exit was the next exit down the road. We need to turn around

A blessed person looks happy.

on life's highway and go back and take the next exit marked 111—one for the Father, one for the Son, and one for the Holy Ghost. The choice is ours.

Get on the Good Foot

We're not happy and blessed because we're out of step with God. God is calling cadence on the right foot but we're keeping time on the left foot. God is saying, "Right foot, right foot, right foot," and we're saying, "Left foot, left foot, left foot." We're out of step. God is saying, "Good foot, good foot, good foot," and we're saying, "Wrong foot, wrong foot, wrong foot."

> Many of us are not blessed because we're walking on the wrong side of the road. We took the wrong exit off life's highway.

However, God is calling us to get on the good foot. If we're out of step, then skip, turn right, and go straight. God wants those of us who are on the wrong foot to get on the good foot, skip, turn right, and go straight.

Color Him Blessed

What is a blessed man like? We should look at the picture. God does not tell us anything about this man except that he's blessed. We don't even know his name. We don't know whether he's a black man or a white man. We don't know whether he's an old man or a young man. We don't know if he's educated or uneducated, whether he has a degree or does not have a degree. We don't know whether he's tall or short. We don't know whether he's handsome or ugly. God just paints him blessed. God simply colors him blessed.

Characteristics of a Blessed Man

As we look at the mirror of reflection, we see three characteristics of a blessed man. First, a blessed man does not willfully, progressively sin. The text says, *"Blessed is the man that walketh not in the counsel of the ungodly, nor standeth in the way of sinners nor sitteth in the seat of the scornful."* The term "walking" in the Bible is a symbol of behavior. Scripture continuously tells us how to walk and how not to walk (Romans 8:1 - KJV).

> A blessed man does not willfully, progressively sin.

One way to define a man who walketh not in the counsel of the ungodly is to picture a man who does. Picture the man in Psalm 1:1 as an unblessed, unhappy, unrighteous man. He walks after the counsel of the ungodly. He walks, meaning he begins to act the way they do. He starts buying into the world's way of thinking. He thinks nothing is wrong with smoking a little joint; it won't cause anything but cancer. After all, cigarettes will do that.

The ungodly may say we are consenting adults and fornication and adultery does not apply to consenting adults. Or they agree that using condoms rather than abstinence is a solution to safe sex; or anger is a natural emotion so it's all right if we go berserk on our children or our spouse when they make a mistake. These are descriptions of walking after the ungodly.

God is not in the mess-blessing business.

God is not in the mess-blessing business. God does not bless sin. God will not bless our mess. A blessed man walketh not with the ungodly nor stands in the path of the sinner. When we walk like they do, we begin to act and think like they do; when we stand in the path of the sinner, we feel comfortable in sin. A blessed man is never comfortable in sin. A blessed man walketh not after the ungodly nor standeth in the path of sinners nor sitteth in the seat of the scornful. Sitting in the seat of the scornful means we become a leading component of wicked ways. In other words, we're leading others to sin. In other words, we're preaching sin. When we're walking, we're acting in sin.

When we're standing, we're feeling comfortable in sin. When we're sitting, we are promoting sin. But a blessed man walketh not, standeth not, and sitteth not in sin. A blessed man walketh not in the counsel of the ungodly nor standeth in the path of sinners.

Second, a man becomes blessed not by seeking prosperity but by seeking righteousness. *"But his delight is in the law of the Lord; and in his law doth he meditate day and night."* Many biblical scholars contribute this psalm to Solomon and not to David. Some people say it's David. I concur with the many who say the writer is Solomon, the son of David. Remember that Solomon was one of the richest men in the world. But in the Bible, we find that Solomon did not ask for riches. Solomon asked for wisdom and God made him rich. We don't prosper by seeking prosperity; we prosper by seeking after righteousness. *"But seek ye first the kingdom of God, and his righteousness; and all these [other] things shall be added unto you"* (Matthew 6:33 - KJV).

> A blessed man walketh not, standeth not, and sitteth not in sin.

> A man becomes blessed not by seeking prosperity but by seeking righteousness.

Third, a blessed man is like a tree. Why a tree? Why not the sun that is the king of the day? Why not the moon that is the queen of the night? Why not the stars that are like twinkling fresh-cut diamonds in the middle of the blue night sky? Why not the mountains that stand so majestic? Why not the ocean blue? But God said a blessed man is like a tree. I'm reminded of the poet who wrote, "I think that I shall never see a poem as lovely as a tree. Poems are made by fools like me but only God can make a tree."

Why a Tree?

God said a blessed man is like a tree because a tree is planted. If we want to be blessed, we must be planted. We must be positioned in the body of Christ. We have to be planted so we can bloom where we are planted. If we want to be blessed, we have to be planted in the family. We have to be planted in the church. We have to be planted in the body. Many of us are not blessed because we are not

A blessed man is like a tree.

planted and positioned right. Some plants and trees grow better in sunlight and others in the shade. Some trees grow better in cold weather, and others in hot weather. Some require much water, and some require very little water. We must be planted in the right position in the body of Christ to be truly blessed right.

We are never planted accidentally in the family of God. A blessed person has been intentionally planted in the family of God. A blessed person shall be like a tree planted by the rivers of water, fertilized and irrigated by Him who is the living water that bringeth forth fruit in his season. So, a blessed person is like a tree that's not only planted but is also productive because he produces fruit in his season. If we are planted right and if we are watered right, we will produce right.

A blessed person is like a tree that's not only planted but is also productive because he produces fruit in his season.

If we don't feel blessed, maybe it's not our season. The text says the blessed man will be fruitful in his season. We must not give up. Our season is coming. This might be my season. This might be his season. This might be her season. But your season is coming. We need to understand that all God's righteous children have a season. Hold on until your season comes. Keep walking by faith. Walk not with the ungodly. Stand not with sinners. Sit not with the scornful. But delight in the Lord and you shall be planted like a tree by the rivers of water that bringeth forth fruit in his season. Hold on for your season.

Not only is a blessed man like a tree because he is planted and productive but also because he is preserved.

God said he will be like a tree. He's planted, productive and preserved. He'll be like a tree planted by the rivers of water that shall bring forth fruit and his leaf shall not wither. He's preserved. He'll be blessed eternally. If we are blessed like a tree, we are not just blessed for a little while, but blessed forever.

Do we remember when mama or maybe grandmama used to make preserves? She would pick apples, peaches or pears off the tree and make preserves. She would put up the preserves so we could eat them later. God says a blessed man's fruit will be preserved for later and forever. We are like a tree now, but there is a crown laid up for us. We can say, like Paul, "*I have fought a good fight, I finished my course, I have kept the faith: Henceforth there is laid up for me a crown of righteousness*" (2 Timothy 4:7–8a - KJV).

A blessed man is like a tree because he is planted and productive but also because he is preserved.

Therefore, "whatsoever he doeth he shall prosper." If we are planted, if we are productive, and if we are preserved, whatever our vocational choice is, we shall prosper. Whether we choose to be a school teacher, CPA, lawyer, doctor or janitor, we will prosper if we are planted, productive and preserved.

On a personal note, I'm glad God told me I can be like a tree. For it was a tree that delivered me. It was on a tree that my sins were washed away. I'm glad I can be like a tree because when I messed up it was on a tree that I got cleaned up. It's interesting how God works. Some of the same things that mess you up can clean you up. It was a tree that messed me up and it was a tree that cleaned me up. It was a woman, a man and a tree that messed me up. The woman was named Eve, and the man was named Adam and it was a tree in the Garden of Eden.

I got messed up in the Garden by a tree, but I'm glad there was yet another tree, another woman and another man. This woman was named Mary and she had a baby that grew up like in stature that found favor with man and God, and the tree was the old rugged

We will prosper if we are planted, productive, and preserved.

cross. I'm glad there was a tree that cleaned me up. Jesus hung on a tree on Golgotha's hill. He bled on a tree. He died on a tree. But I'm glad the story doesn't stop there. The Bible says early Sunday morning He got up with all power in His hands. I love that old tree.

Was it for crimes that I had done? He groaned upon the tree. Amazing pity, grace unknown and love beyond degree. At the cross (at the tree) where I first saw the light and the burden of my heart rolled away.

It was there by faith I received my sight and now I am blessed, now I am happy!

Summary

In Psalm 1, God shows us a picture, a double image of what a blessed and unblessed person looks like so we can make the right choice and be blessed. The major thrust is on a model blessed man. The image of a model blessed man is shown as 1) one who does not willfully, progressively sin; 2) one who does not seek prosperity, but rather seeks righteousness; and 3) one who is blessed like a tree. A tree that is intentionally planted in the family and body of Christ. A tree that, in season, is nurtured, and in due season is productive and fruitful. Also, a tree that is preserved and eternally blessed. Like a tree, we who are planted and nurtured, productive, fruitful and preserved will prosper (be blessed) regardless of our place in life.

CHAPTER EIGHTEEN

Blessed Through Your Calling

1 Peter 3:8–12 (RSV)

8 *Finally, all of you, have unity of spirit, sympathy, love of the brethren, a tender heart and a humble mind.*

9 *Do not return evil for evil or reviling for reviling; but on the contrary bless, for to this you have been called, that you may obtain a blessing.*

10 *For "He that would love life and see good days, let him keep his tongue from evil and his lips from speaking guile;*

11 *Let him turn away from evil and do right; let him seek peace and pursue it.*

12 *For the eyes of the Lord are upon the righteous, and his ears are open to their prayer.*

But the face of the Lord is against those that do evil.

Blessed Through Your Calling

Let me call your attention to verse 9 in the referenced scripture: "... *for to this you have been called, that you may obtain a blessing.*" The King James Version says that we have been called "to inherit a blessing." When He saved us, God called us to inherit a blessing.

There is a blessing that belongs especially to each of us. Scripture says that we have been called to inherit a blessing. There is a blessing with our name on it. If we are not careful, we will miss our blessing.

Blessings do not come in generalities. We are not just generally blessed. Often we speak of blessings in general terms; we just want to be generally blessed. But God does not always, and most often does not, bless us generally. We have been called. We have been called to inherit a blessing.

Blessing must be defined according to individual purpose and divine directions. Not understanding this concept will cause us to be forever frustrated trying to be blessed like somebody else. We will be frustrated trying to be successful like somebody else, thinking that we're not blessed when comparing our blessings with others. Some parents are frustrated because their child is not as successful, by

God called us to inherit a blessing.

their definition, as their neighbor's child, or as their best friend's child. We need to understand that the purpose for our children may not be *our* purpose. God may have another purpose for each of our children that's different from that of our neighbor's child.

What Is God's Purpose for You

We cannot talk about blessings without talking about individual purpose and Holy Ghost guidance. The question then is, "What is God's purpose for you?" Whatever His purpose for you is, He has gifted you accordingly. Therefore, if you discover your gift, you will discover your purpose and will be blessed. The Bible says that if God has saved you, He has spiritually gifted you.

> Whatever His purpose for us is, He has gifted us accordingly. Therefore, if we discover our gift, we will discover our purpose and we will be blessed.

We should not confuse our spiritual gifts with our talents. We had our talents when we were born, but we do not receive our spiritual gift(s) until we were born again. Some of us may have been talented athletes or talented musicians, but when we were born again, God gifted us spiritually for a purpose and a task. Therefore, if we discover our gift(s), we will discover our purpose and we will be blessed.

Missed Blessings

The question arises, "What's keeping many of us from being blessed?" 1 Peter warns us to do good and not evil so we won't miss our blessing. The Lord loves righteousness and the Lord turns His face on evil. To be blessed, we must seek righteousness and avoid evil.

To be blessed, we must seek righteousness and avoid evil.

"*But seek ye first the kingdom of God, and his righteousness; and all these things shall be added unto you*" (Matthew 6:33 - KJV). Seek means to look for. Seek means not just to be good, but to look for good. We need to seek righteousness before we can obtain the blessing that has our name on it.

Too Evil to Be Blessed

This scripture tells us the number one weapon of an evil person is the tongue. The tongue has it's own world of iniquity. The tongue, which is as dangerous as lust, has its own subculture of iniquity and this subculture of iniquity loves the church. Many believers have been delivered from the sin of lust, but the world of iniquity of the tongue is living well among the saints in the church.

The Tongue: A Blessing or a Curse

The question is, "Will we bless others with our tongue or will we curse others with our tongues?" If we know our tongue has not been a blessing to others, we need to fall on our face and repent before the Lord God Almighty.

In the Old Testament, God had given Balaam the ability to curse or bless effectively. The enemy of God, king of the Moabite tribe, Balak, knew that Balaam had the power in his tongue to curse or bless. So Balak hired Balaam to curse the Israelites because God had made them mighty (Numbers 22 & 24).

But Balaam didn't take the money. He wanted to talk to God about it. God told Balaam that these were His people and not to curse them, but bless them.

Then the king of the Moabites sent others to talk to Balaam again, and he offered Balaam more money. He offered Balaam riches—the wages of unright-

Many believers have been delivered from the sin of lust, but the world of iniquity of the tongue is living well among the saints in the church.

eousness. He offered him silver and gold. This time Balaam again said I need to check with God before I take this money, but God knew Balaam's heart and that he had the money in his eyes.

God had to meet Balaam in a special way. God met him with a dumb ass, a donkey, and stopped him in his tracks before making a mistake. Balaam, still being eager to be an ambassador for the king of Moab, whipped his donkey and the donkey cried out, "Why are you whipping me? I haven't done anything. It's your problem. You're the one in love with this money." The donkey talked; the dumb ass talked to a dumb person. Sometimes we need a dummy to talk to a dummy. The donkey said, "I'm not in love with the money, you're in love with the money. Why are you whipping me?" God works in mysterious ways.

Balaam sought the Lord again, and this time the Lord told him not only do we not curse them but also we want to bless the people of Israel. So Balaam gave four blessings. By the time he got to the fourth blessing, the enemy of God was irate with Balaam and said if you're not going to curse them, whatever you do just don't bless them.

Our lives mirror Balaam in many ways. Many of us are in love with the wages of unrighteousness. But God is calling us today, wherever we might be in our journey, to stop and repent of our cursing tongues. We must prepare to receive the blessing with our name on it.

We should never say anything about anybody unless it helps them. We should not tell about deacon so-and-so who's getting a divorce. Is that helping him? Is giving me that information helping him? We should not tell that sister so-and-so's daughter is pregnant. We say, "Well, I'm telling the truth." That's not the question. We say, "I'm giving information, I'm not gossiping." If it is not helping, it is a curse. The only time we should mention another person in conversation is when it helps that person.

> *We should never say anything about anybody unless it helps them.*

In some cases our evil is deceptive. We approach people and say, "I want you to pray with me about brother so-and-so." Here comes the curse, now—in the form of a prayer. "He's having problems in his marriage. Let's pray for him right now." We need a donkey or something dumb or intelligent to stop us in our path and cause us to repent. If we want to be blessed, we must turn our tongues into instruments of blessing.

Give Up Retaliation

God's Word says if we don't want to miss our blessing, we have to give up retaliation. Retaliation is doing evil for evil: "I'm going to talk about her because she talked about me. I'm going to talk about him because the world's been bad to me." We can't do evil for evil and expect to find favor with God.

If we want to be blessed, we must turn our tongue into an instrument of blessing.

Our flesh wants to retaliate. We can't retaliate if we want to be blessed.

God's Word says that we have to give up retaliation. We cannot do evil for evil and still have the blessing that has our name on it. We have been called to inherit a blessing. As long as we do evil for evil, as long as we retaliate on every evil that comes our way, we are avoiding that blessing with our name on it.

Pursue Peace

Scripture says if we don't want to miss our blessing, we have to pursue peace. In other words, we must run after peace. Peace and our blessings are integrally connected. It doesn't matter how badly people treat us, we still have to run after peace. The scripture says *pursue* peace, not just *have* peace. Just go after it. No matter how people talk about us or mistreat us, we must run after peace. If we chase peace, we'll catch our blessing.

Don't Switch Price Tags

Don't miss your blessing by trying to change the price tag on the blessing. God is watching you; His eye is upon you. Some of us, before God cleansed us, would go in the store and see the price tag on one suit and try to put that tag on another suit. Some of us used to see a price tag on one dress and, because nobody was looking, we would take the price tag off that dress and put it on another dress. This dress is the one we really want, but it costs too much, so we would switch price tags. Some of us are doing that with our blessings. We're trying to take the price tag off. It costs to be blessed. There's a price tag on every blessing.

> We cannot do evil for evil and still have the blessing that has our name on it.

If we want to be blessed, we must stop trying to change the price tag. The blessing we are called to receive based on God's purpose for us may cost more than another blessing. We should not change the price tag because we may be giving it to somebody else when blessing belongs to us. If we want to be blessed, whatever we do, we must not change the name on the gift.

We used to do that under the Christmas tree. When one box looked a little bigger than the other, we would take our name off that little box and put it on the bigger box. No, that other box is yours, that's your blessing, that's your gift. It's your blessing according to your calling. Don't try to change the names. Stop comparing blessings. We can't compare blessings because our blessings are in accordance with God's purpose for our life.

God has chosen us for a blessing. He has called us to inherit our blessing. We must claim our blessing.

Summary

If we have experienced grace, we have been called to inherit a blessing. Blessings do not come in generalities. If we are not careful, we can miss a blessing with our name on it. Blessings must be defined according to individual purpose and divine direction. Whatever God's purpose is, He has gifted us accordingly. Therefore, when we operate in our spiritual gifts, we discover our purpose, and we will be blessed. In order to be blessed we must seek righteousness and avoid evil.

Our tongues can either be an instrument of a blessing or a curse. We cannot do evil for evil and still have

There's a price tag on every blessing. If we want to be blessed, we must stop trying to change the price tag.

the blessing that God has prepared for us. If we want to be blessed, we must make our tongues an instrument of blessing. Also, if we don't want to miss the blessing of our calling, we must pursue peace. If we chase peace, we will catch our blessings. In addition, there is a price tag on every blessing. We cannot change the price tag on our blessing

We can't compare blessings because our blessings are in accordance with God's purpose for our life.

because it costs too much. God has called us to receive the blessing with our name on it. If we switch price tags, we might give away the blessing we have been called to receive.

CHAPTER NINETEEN

Blessed Through the Gospel of Forgiveness

Psalm 32:1–2 (KJV)

¹ Blessed is he whose transgression is forgiven, whose sin is covered.
² Blessed is the man unto whom the LORD imputeth not iniquity, and in whose spirit there is no guile.

We're blessed through and by the gospel. The gospel is what we preach. The gospel is the Good News that Christ died for the forgiveness of our sins. It's the Good News that God robed himself in flesh in the person of his Son, Jesus, died for the remission of our sin and the sin of the world, and was raised on the third day for our justification so that our faith can be counted as righteousness. He also ascended into heaven and is now sitting on the right hand of God the Father until He comes again to judge both the living and the dead. Until that day, He is with us in the person of the Holy Spirit. That's the gospel. And we are blessed by the gospel through the power of God's forgiveness.

A Gospel Psalm

I find Psalm 32 to be a most interesting psalm in that it is a gospel psalm. It is a doctrine psalm. Not many of the 150 psalms give the gospel or have any doctrine connection. David is the author and beside his name is the Hebrew word *Maschil*. That is a Hebrew word that means instruction; so, this psalm is a psalm of instruction. It instructs us how we're blessed through and by the gospel. This psalm teaches us about the doctrine of sin, the doctrine of repentance, and the doctrine of forgiveness. This psalm instructs us how we are blessed through forgiveness and what ought to be our appropriate response.

We are blessed by the gospel through the power of God's forgiveness.

Notice it opens on a high note and closes on a high note. It opens with two Beatitudes. It says, *"Blessed is he whose transgression is forgiven, whose sin is covered."* A second Beatitude follows, *"Blessed is the man unto whom the Lord imputeth not iniquity, and in whose spirit there is no guile."* Then it closes in verse 11 by saying, *"Be glad in the Lord, and rejoice, ye righteous: and shout for joy."* In other words, if we have experienced what David has experienced in the forgiveness of our sins, we ought to be glad about it and rejoice and shout for joy. This is a marvelous instruction God has given us.

Repentance is necessary for forgiveness. If there is no repentance, there is no forgiveness. We are blessed by forgiveness itself.

Repentance is necessary for forgiveness. If there is no repentance, there is no forgiveness. We are blessed by forgiveness itself. If we are not blessed in any other way, we are blessed because of God's forgiveness. We ought to be glad enough about it to shout for joy.

The Psalmist and His Experience

What makes this psalm powerful is that it was written from the experience of its author, David. Most biblical scholars feel that David wrote this after his experience with the prophet Nathan that led him to repent of his sins with Bathsheba and Uriah.

Many of us resemble David. As I mentioned before, David is on record as the greatest sinner and the greatest saint of the Old Testament. That's an interesting combination. Although little David played his harp and although little David killed big Goliath, he grew up to become King David and took advantage of his kingship by having an adulterous affair with Bathsheba. Even though I told this story before in a previous chapter, I must tell it again so that you understand the power of God's forgiveness. Bathsheba was married to Uriah, a captain of David's army. She was a Hittite married to a Hittite, Uriah, from the Hamitic tribe. David committed adultery with her and tried to cover it up by sending Uriah to the front line of battle where he would be killed. David was an adulterer and a murderer.

Many of us resemble David.

David tried to hide his sin, but God would not let him go. Aren't we glad that sometimes God won't let us go? We may try to hide, but God's so good He just won't let us go. David said, "Thy hand was heavy upon me."

God sent the prophet Nathan to David to tell David a story of an ewe little lamb (2 Samuel 12). There was

244

a rich man who had many lambs and a poor man who had only one little ewe lamb. This only lamb was like a child in his house. The lamb ate with them and slept by the bed with them. A traveler came to the rich man and rather than getting a lamb from his many, the rich man took the poor man's little lamb and slaughtered it for the traveler. David heard the story, pulled out his sword, and said, "Where is he? This man should die."

Nathan pointed his hand to David and said, *"David, thou art the man"* (2 Samuel 12:7 - KJV). In other words, Nathan said, "David, that's what you did when you took Uriah's wife into your own chamber." David confessed and repented and said to Nathan, *"I have sinned against the Lord"* (2 Samuel 12:13 - KJV). Nathan said unto David, *"The Lord also hath put away thy sin; thou shall not die"* (2 Samuel 12:13 - KJV). To die means to go to hell. It's appointed once for every man to die. Nathan said, "The Lord has put away your sin, David; thou shall not go to hell."

An Interpretation

Sometime later, David wrote Psalm 32: *"Blessed is he whose transgression is forgiven, whose sin is covered. Blessed is the man unto whom the Lord imputeth not iniquity, and in whose spirit there is no guile. When I kept silence, my bones waxed old through my roaring all day long. For day and night thy hand was heavy upon me: my moisture is turned into the drought of the summer. Selah. I acknowledged my sins unto thee, and mine iniquity have I not hid. I said, I will confess my transgressions unto the Lord; and thou forgavest the iniquity of my sin. Selah. . . . Thou art my hiding place; thou shalt preserve me from trouble; thou shalt compass me about with songs of deliverance. Selah."*

Selah means to stop, look, and listen. It's a musical rest. At times we have music played and then it says, "Stop." Selah says, "He has taken, has hidden my sins; He has covered my sins." Selah. In other words, just stop and resonate here a bit. David said, "Let me stop, look back, and think about the goodness of the Lord." In other words, "Let me park here and just give some praise." It's a musical rest, but it's a time to rejoice. Let me just look back over my shoulders. When I look back over my life and I think things over, I can truly say that I've been blessed. I have a testimony. Selah means stop, park, and look at the goodness of God; look from where He's brought us.

Selah means stop, park, and look at the goodness of God; look from where He's brought us.

David says he's blessed because his transgressions are forgiven. His sin is covered and the Lord imputeth not his iniquity. The biblical concept of sin is revealed from three perspectives. One is that sin is noted by the word, "transgression." Transgression means breaking away from God's law; rebellion. The second is the meaning of the word "sin." The Hebrew word for sin means error or missing the mark. The third is "iniquity." It has a different meaning. It means pervert or depravity with the whole idea of a burden of guilt.

Guilty by Resemblance

David says he's guilty of all three. We resemble David because some of us, like David, are guilty. We need to stop and park here a while. All have sinned and fallen short of the glory of God. *"If we say that we have no sin, we deceive ourselves, and the truth is not in us. If we say that we have not sinned, we make him a liar, and his word is not in us"* (1 John 1:8–10 - KJV). We may not have murdered anybody, but if we hate our brother, according to Jesus, we are murderers (Matthew 5:21–22). We may not have committed adultery with Bathsheba, but if we have ever looked on another with lust, we have committed adultery in our hearts (Matthew 5:28). If we say we have no sin, we deceive ourselves and the truth is not in us. But, thank God, *"If we confess our sins, he is faithful and just to forgive* us of our sins, and to cleanse us of from all unrighteousness" (1 John 1:9 - KJV).

Sin Committed and Sin Concealed

David treats sin in a very special way. He walks us through stages of his sin. First, he says, "I did it." If he were forgiven, forgiveness implies that it had to be done. Sin was committed. Then, David concealed his sin. David said, "I kept silent." I wonder how long David would have kept silent if God had not sent the prophet Nathan to him? Aren't we glad that God will not take his hand off us? I wonder how long many of us would have kept silent if God had not sent someone with a word for us?

> God loves us so much that when we sin, He's not going to take His hand off us.

God loves us so much that when we sin, He's not going to take His hand off of us. An unsaved person can sin and really get away with it, as far as his conscience goes. But if we know the Lord and have ever experienced His grace, when we sin, God is so good to us that He's not going to let us get away with it. He's going to send us an opportunity to repent. Aren't we glad that He, instead of man, is our judge? I'll take Judge Jesus over Judge Judy any day. Aren't we glad

248

Judge Judy or any other human judge is not on the throne?

Sin's Burden

David said he was walking around with this heavy burden on him. It's a burden of guilt that causes us to know we are wrong. This burden of guilt is like a rock on our shoulders. It's bending us over. We become bent over in our hearts and in our souls because of sin's burden of guilt.

Sin Confessed

David said we ought to do as he did. This is an instruction. David said, *"I acknowledged my sin unto thee, and my iniquity have I not hid. I said, I will confess my transgressions unto the Lord; and thou forgavest the iniquity of my sin. Selah"* (Psalm 32:5). God's hand of mercy is upon somebody today. We, like David, need to talk to God about it.

Sin Forgiven

The final way we view sin is as sin forgiven. The forgiveness is greater than the sin. We mentioned three concepts of sin: transgression, breaking away; missing the mark, the error; and the pervasiveness of guilt. The forgiveness is strong enough to overcome sin, any and all concepts of sin.

Views of Forgiveness

There are several views of forgiveness. One of the views of forgiveness is "lifted off, let go." Forgiveness means to lift off and let go. When we lift off some-thing and let go of something, we are set free. If we have a burden, it's lifted off and we are let go, which means we are set free. A second view of forgiveness means "covered." Not only is it lifted off

> There may be much sin, but God has enough forgiveness, enough grace for all the sin in the world.

and let go of, but it's also covered as if a lid or a veil was put over it. It is put out of sight. The third view is "cancellation." Not only does He lift it off and cover our sin, but He also erases it. He cancels it out like it never happened. That's why we say, *greater is he that is in you, than he that is in the world*" (1 John 4:4 - KJV). There may be much sin, but God has enough for-giveness and enough grace for all the sin in the world. He lifted it. He covered it. He erased it. He put it away, never to rise again.

We all are ex-convicts. That may be a hard word for us, but everybody is an ex-con. Ex-cons can hardly get a job in our society. If a serial killer is released and moved into our neighborhood, we want to know about it. If a serial rapist who has been released is living next door to us, we want to know about it. But guess what? God erases our records. We're all ex-cons, but we can move anywhere we want to move. There will never be any record in heaven of our sin. It's been lifted off, it's been let go, it's been covered, it's been canceled, it's been erased, it's been put in the sea of forgetfulness, never to rise again.

> There will never be any record in heaven of our sin.

Our Stubbornness

God says our problem is that some of us are like mules. *"I will instruct thee and teach thee in the way which thou shalt go: I will guide thee with mine eye. Be ye not as the horse, or as the mule, which have no understanding: whose mouth must be held in with bit and bridle, lest they come near unto thee"* (Psalm 32:8–9 - KJV). God humbles us by saying, "Don't be like a horse or a mule with no understanding, whose mouth must be held with a bit and a bridle." Some of us are so stubborn that God has to put a bit and bridle in our mouths to keep us from hurting ourselves and others. God says in verse 8, *"I will guide thee with mine eye."* He said that a person is blessed by forgiveness, and He will guide us by His eye.

God's Loving Guidance

Would we rather have God guide us with a strap around our heads and a bit in our mouths, or by His loving eye? The mule has to be guided by a harness and a bit. The sparrow is guided with the tender eye. The question is, "Are we going to be a mule or a sparrow?" If we are like the sparrow, we can sing the song, "I sing because I'm happy, I sing because I'm blessed. I've been pardoned and I've been set free. I've been forgiven. I've been blessed and forgiven. I've been blessed by the gospel." We are indeed blessed through the gospel of forgiveness.

Some of us are so stubborn that God has to put a bit and bridle in our mouths to keep us from hurting ourselves and others.

Summary

We are blessed through a gospel that has a provision for forgiveness of our sin no matter how great our sins may be. Psalm 32 is an unusual psalm in that it represents the gospel from the psalmist's experiential perspective. The backdrop of Psalm 32 gives us a springboard into identifying with the psalms' author, David. Many believers resemble David. In many ways, David's experience of "sin committed and sin forgiven" is our experience.

Sin is viewed in five stages: 1) sin committed; 2) sin concealed; 3) sin's heavy burden; 4) sin confessed; and 5) sin forgiven. The biblical concept of sin is revealed from three perspectives: 1) transgression, which means to stray away from; 2) sin, which means to miss the mark; and 3) iniquity, which carries with it the burden of guilt. We are blessed because the strength of forgiveness is greater than any sin. Forgiveness also has three views, namely: 1) lifted off and let go; 2) cover up; and 3) erased or canceled.

> *Would we rather have God guide us with a strap around our head and a bit in our mouth, or by His loving eye?*

God stands ready to bless us through forgiveness. We have the choice of being stubborn like a mule that needs a bit in its mouth to be guided by, or like a sparrow that is guided by the loving eye of God. The loving eye of God, through His Word, tells us that if we repent and confess our sins we will be blessed through the gospel of forgiveness.

CHAPTER TWENTY

Blessed Through Blessing the Poor

Psalm 41:1–3 (KJV)

1 *Blessed is he that considereth the poor: the* LORD *will deliver him in time of trouble.*

2 *The* LORD *will preserve him, and keep him alive; and he shall be blessed upon the earth: and thou wilt not deliver him unto the will of his enemies.*

3 *The* LORD *will strengthen him upon the bed of languishing: thou wilt make all his bed in his sickness.*

This chapter teaches us about the blessing associated with giving to those who are poor, oppressed, depressed, suppressed, and in need. God tells us we can be especially blessed by giving to the poor. Also, if we fail to give to the poor, they cry to the Lord against us. "*. . . And thou givest him nought; and he cry unto the* LORD *against thee, and it be sin unto thee*" (Deuteronomy 15:9b - KJV). We don't want the poor crying out against us. The Lord prefers to bless us. God especially blesses those who bless the poor.

Who Are the Poor?

Who are the poor? The poor are those who need help at any present time. As a matter of fact, the way many of us live, from paycheck to paycheck, we may just be one paycheck away from being among the poor. Each time I go to a shelter for the homeless, one of the things I experience is that there are always a few people there who look like us. The rest of the people don't look like us. They are not dressed like us. They don't smell like us. But there are always a few who look just like we do. When I first saw these people who looked like us I would wonder, are they on a mission from another church? But I found out that was not the case. They had just entered the shelter. This was their first

> We can be especially blessed by giving to the poor.

night. After three or four weeks they begin to look like they belong. I would look at someone who had just gotten there, and it would give me a reality check and an attitude of gratitude check. I would say, "If not for the grace of God, there go I."

The poor are those who are in need of help for survival. Sometimes the poor just need to make it through the day. Sometimes the poor just need to make it through the night. God tells us that the poor will always be with us. I don't know what that does for our war on poverty through government programs.

> *God has said to us that the poor will always be with us.*

God has said to us that the poor will always be with us. Don't ever buy into the theology that asserts that God doesn't love the poor. Please don't buy into the preaching of false prophets who say that the reason some people are poor is that they don't have enough faith in God. That is false prophesy. This is not a Word from God. God has a special blessing that He wants for the poor. God loves poor people.

Because the poor will always be with us, this is an opportunity for us to be blessed doubly. It is an opportunity for us to be multiply blessed because God has said that there are blessings for those who bless the poor. Look at the blessings God tells us that we might receive in Psalm 41:1- 3. First of all, God tells us through the psalmist that blessed is the person that considereth the poor. Then it goes on to list some of these blessings.

Blessing One - Deliverance in the Time of Trouble

If we consider the poor, we will be delivered in the time of trouble. I'm glad to know that I will be delivered in the time of trouble. If we don't have any trouble, we haven't lived long enough. Keep living and I guarantee that trouble will come your way. Beecher Hicks says in his book, *Preaching Through the Storm*, that we are either in one of three places. We are either in a storm, going into a storm, or coming out of a storm.

> If we consider the poor, we will be delivered in the time of trouble.

I remember when I read that, we were just getting ready to purchase a facility and I thought to myself, well, I'm not in a storm and I'm not coming out of a storm. If he is right, I must be getting ready to go into a storm. I took heed and started boarding up the windows. We need to start preparing for the storm. We know when a storm comes, we get out the plywood and start boarding up the windows. We need to get out some spiritual plywood in our lives and start

258

boarding up the windows. If there is no storm in our lives now, we need to be well assured that there is a storm on the way. The Bible says that if we bless the poor, He will deliver us in the time of trouble.

Blessing Two - Numbering Your Days to Be on Earth

If we bless the poor, the Lord will keep us alive long enough to bless us on earth. Isn't that a wonderful thing to know. But many of us do not consider our-selves truly blessed here on earth. We might be saying that we are not blessed like we would like to be blessed. We need to know something. God has made a

> *If we bless the poor, the Lord will keep us alive long enough to bless us on earth.*

promise. If we bless the poor, He will number our days long enough for us to give testimony that we are blessed here on the earth. There ought to be some hope in that for somebody.

Blessing Three - Deliverance From Your Enemy

If we bless the poor, the Lord will not deliver us into the hands of your enemy. Sometimes God in His permissive will allows the devil to touch us. Remember Job? It was only through God's permissive will that the devil touched His servant, Job. But the Lord is saying if we bless the poor, He will never deliver us into the hands of our enemies. We don't have to go through what Job went through.

Blessing Four - Strength When You are Sick

If we bless the poor, He will strengthen us on our sick bed. Have we ever been sick? Well if we haven't, we need to just keep living. There may come a day when we will be on the bed of languishing. When we are on the bed of affliction, it is good to know that we have some blessings in the bank. God is calling us to put some blessings in the bank so that when we are on our sick bed, the Holy Ghost can make a withdrawal on our behalf. It is good to have some blessings in the bank. We need to bless the poor, so we can bank some blessings in our time of sickness.

> If you bless the poor, I will not deliver you into the hands of your enemy.

Insensitivity Caused by Lack of Gratitude

Our problem is simply our insensitivity due to a lack of gratitude. Many of us will sit down at the Thanksgiving table and will not remember the poor. We will not remember and thank God for from where He has brought us. God has brought us from a mighty long way.

God reminded the people of Israel, His called out ones, throughout the Old Testament that when they came into the land and were full, to not forget the Lord their God who brought them out of bondage. Today we are sitting in houses we did not build; we are driving cars that we did not create. We are eating food that we did not man-

We need to bless the poor, so we can bank some blessings.

ufacture. So when we eat, and are full, we need to remember the Lord our God and how far He has brought us.

More Blessed to Give Than Receive

In Acts 20:35, God said that it is more blessed to give than to receive. We need to ask ourselves this question. On which end of the equation would we rather be? Would we rather be on the giving side, or would we rather be on the receiving side? Some of us need to be more active in social ministries. We need to visit the homeless shelter more often. We need to go on foreign mission trips. We need to see some third world countries, or better still, some fourth world countries. I saw Gambia several summers ago. I wouldn't call it a third world country, but a fourth world country. A peaceful country by the way, but a very very poor country with living conditions some of us can't even imagine. We need to understand, somehow, just how blessed we are. It is more blessed to give than to receive.

> It is more blessed to give than to receive.

Blessing God by Blessing the Poor

When we bless the poor according to the Word of God, we bless the person of Jesus Christ. Matthew 25:37–40 clearly says, *"Then shall the righteous answer him, saying, Lord, when saw we thee an hungred, and fed thee? or thirsty, and gave thee drink? When saw we thee a stranger, and took thee in? or naked, and clothed thee? Or when saw we thee sick, or in prison, and came unto thee? And the King shall answer and say unto them, Verily I say unto you, Inasmuch as ye have done it unto one of the least of these my brethren, ye have done it unto me."*

Jesus said feed the hungry, clothe the naked, give drink to the thirsty. Those who do not do this are the goats. The others who do this are the sheep. Then the question came up, when did we ever see you thirsty and did not give you drink Master? The goats were terrified. Master Jesus, please tell us when did we ever see you hungry and did not feed you? When Jesus? We never saw you in prison and did not visit you. Lord, please tell us. Master, you know if I had ever seen you

When we bless the poor according to the word of God, we bless the person of Jesus Christ.

naked, I would have clothed you. Jesus said that when we fail to do it unto the least of our brethren, we fail to do it unto Him. When we did it unto the least of them, we did it unto the Lord. The next poor person we see, we need to realize upon whom we are looking.

A Nightmare as a Testimony

God works with me in mysterious and strange ways. I remember when I refused a poor, peg-legged man in downtown Atlanta when I was teaching at Georgia State University. This person asked me for some money to buy some food, and I refused him. I said in my mind that he only wants to get a drink of whiskey. Then after I walked away I heard the Word of God speak to me: "When you have done unto the least of these you have done it also unto me." I literally turned around to try to find the peg-legged man. He was running to catch a bus, and he was running faster on his peg-leg it seemed, than I could run on my good legs. He got on the bus, and I was trying to give him something when the bus pulled off. I ran behind the bus for approximately a half block before I was exhausted. Once in a while still, I wake up in the middle of the night in a cold sweat running behind a bus with these words resonating and resounding in my soul: "When you have done it unto the least of these my brethren, you have also done it unto me." God has blessed me with this nightmare as a testimony. He doesn't have to worry about me anymore. I will never let a poor man go by. If he wants to buy some whiskey with it, that's his problem. I don't want the poor crying out against me.

> Giving to the poor puts a spark of gratitude in our attitude.

A Spark of Gratitude in Your Attitude

If we are thoughtful, we will be thankful. If we will consider the poor, we will be thankful for what God has already done for us. Giving to the poor puts a spark of gratitude in our attitude. The problem is that many of us do not have an attitude of gratitude. In my family we have a tradition of letting our children make their Christmas wish lists. We had the hardest time convincing our youngest son that his list had to be cut. A strange thing happened. My wife and I, along with our youngest son, went down to the homeless shelter with our Social Ministry. My wife and I had been working with our son and this long list that he didn't want cut. Well, we went down and were feeding the people. I noticed how perplexed he was. Finally, he asked me, "Daddy, where is their stuff?" I asked him what he meant by their stuff. He said, "their things, their stuff." I said, "All they have is what they have on their backs, son, and maybe a little bag tied up with a knot. That's their stuff." One of the most miraculous things happened that Christmas his is still a part of the essence of that young man. On that Christmas his long list disappeared. He never mentioned it again. He did receive a few things for Christmas, but that list never came up again.

Some of us need to experience something so that our list will disappear. We ask God to bless us with a list of things—I want this, and I want that. We need to go down and visit with the poor for a little while. We need to go and spend some time at the shelter, and we will realize how blessed we really are. Simply put, we need to count our blessings. Though we are blessed,

God has promised in His Word that we can be especially blessed by blessing the poor.

Summary

God promises that we will be especially blessed by offering a helping hand and by giving to the poor. God warns us that if we fail to help the poor, the poor may testify against us before the Lord. The poor are those who need help to survive at any given time. God has said that the poor will always be with us. Poor people are not poor because God does not love them or because they lack faith. Because the poor will always be with us, we have the opportunity to be especially blessed. We can bless the poor and be multiply blessed. God, speaking to us through the psalmist, promises us that if we bless the poor, we will 1) experience deliverance in the time of trouble, 2) live long enough to be blessed on earth, 3) be delivered from our enemies, and 4) be strengthened when we are sick.

We forfeit our blessings by not blessing the poor. Our lack of gratitude has made us insensitive. To overcome our insensitivity, we must put some gratitude in our attitude by remembering that it is more blessed to give than to receive. We need to know that when we give to the poor, we give to the person of Jesus. An extra spark of gratitude will become a part of our attitudes if we simply count our blessings.

CHAPTER TWENTY-ONE

Blessed Through Fasting and Praying

Matthew 6:16–18 (KJV)

16 *Moreover when ye fast, be not, as the hypocrites, of a sad countenance: for they disfigure their faces, that they may appear unto men to fast. Verily I say unto you, They have their reward.*

17 *But thou, when thou fastest, anoint thine head, and wash thy face;*

18 *That thou appear not unto men to fast, but unto thy Father which is in secret: and thy Father, which seeth in secret, shall reward thee openly.*

I believe, based on personal experience with the Word of God and the Spirit of God, that fasting appropriately (according to scripture) coupled with praying appropriately (according to scripture) is a nuclear bomb ready to explode into gigantic blessings.

As indicated repeatedly throughout this book, I am a blessed man and a living testimony to the goodness of God. Recently, just in the last ten years, I discovered the blessings God has for His children through fasting. I believe there are many believers who know and have experienced the power and blessings that come through prayer, but have yet to discover the blessings that come through fasting. Most believers know that prayer changes things, and prayer changes people. We are familiar with the cliche, "No prayer, no power; little prayer, little power; much prayer, much power." God says in Matthew 6:6 (KJV) that if we pray as He has taught us to pray we will be rewarded. *"But thou, when thou prayest, enter into thy closet, and when thou hast shut thy door, pray to thy Father which is in secret; and thy Father which seeth in secret shall reward thee openly."*

Divinely sandwiched between Matthew 6:1–7, which speaks to us concerning the blessing of praying right, and Matthew 6:16–18, which teaches us concerning the blessing of fasting right, is the model prayer Jesus taught us to pray called "The Lord's Prayer." Also, these scriptures are a part of a larger scripture narrative referred to as Jesus' "Sermon on the Mount" which includes the blessed teaching of the "Beatitudes." I think the setting and the background of these scriptures are significant because they reinforce the truth that God really wants us to know, that we can be mightily blessed through fasting and praying. These inspired words are from the lips of Jesus. Jesus is saying read my lips, "I want to bless you."

A Personal Challenge and Formula for Being Blessed through Fasting and Praying

I want to offer a personal challenge to every reader of *How to Be Blessed* to indeed be blessed through praying and fasting. I dare you and even double dare you to try this simple formula for being blessed for just ten days in three consecutive months. To assure you are praying according to scripture, choose a biblical model prayer. I am suggesting three to choose from. First, you may choose the "Lord's Prayer" as recorded in Matthew 6:9–13 (KJV): *"Our Father which art in heaven, Hallowed be thy name. Thy kingdom come. Thy will be done in earth, as it is in heaven. Give us this day our daily bread. And forgive us our debts, as we forgive our debtors. And lead us not into temptation, but deliver us from evil: For thine is the kingdom, and the* power, and the glory, for ever. Amen." Or you may choose to pray Paul's prayer found in Ephesians 3:14–19 (KJV): *"For this cause I bow my knees unto the Father of our Lord Jesus Christ, Of whom the whole family in heaven and earth is named, That he would grant you, according to the riches of his glory, to be strengthened with might by his Spirit in the inner man; That Christ may dwell in your hearts by faith; that ye, being rooted and grounded in love, May be able to comprehend with all saints what is the breadth, and length, and depth, and height; And to know the love of Christ, which passeth knowledge, that ye might be filled with all the fulness of God."*

Finally, you may choose to pray the simple, but powerful prayer of Jabez, couched in the Old Testament book of 1 Chronicles 4:9,10 (KJV): *"And Jabez was more honourable than his brethren: and his mother called his name Jabez, saying, Because I bare him with sorrow. And Jabez called on the God of Israel, saying, Oh that thou wouldest bless me indeed, and enlarge my coast, and that thine hand might be with me, and that thou wouldest keep me from evil, that it may not grieve me! And God granted him that which he requested."*

Remember, our purpose is to pray according to God's will, so we should pray the biblical model prayers word for word as they were inspired by God. The key is to pray them in faith, expecting and behaving like God has already answered, "Yes," to our requests. In addition, we must keep in mind what we learned in the introduction of this book and that is, the key factor is in the asking.

Couple either of these prayers with a fast. I am suggesting that you fast by abstaining from any solid food (water and juices allowed) from either 6 A.M. to 6 P.M., or 6 P.M. to 6 A.M. Choose the time interval that is most sacrificial for you according to your established eating patterns. If you are primarily an evening eater choose to fast during the evening interval of 6 P.M. to 6 A.M. However, if you are like most people who eat breakfast, lunch and dinner daily, choose the daytime hours of 6 A.M. to 6 P.M. A word of caution, do not change or alter these times in any manner to accommodate situational circumstances or responsibilities. Also, read and adhere to the rest of this chapter on fasting to assure that your fast will be in accordance with God's Word and will.

You are now ready to accept the challenge to be blessed through praying and fasting. Engage yourself in praying and fasting and watch your blessings begin to flow. Do this consistently, and constantly, for ten days out of each of the next three months and your life will never be the same. You will have discovered the power of fasting and praying.

A Personal Inspiration to Fast and Pray

I received an inspiration from God, which can be validated in His Word. He told me that our responsibility in praying is not complete unless we also fast. Therefore, the focus of this chapter will be more on fasting than on praying. God says in His Word to pray and fast. There are various levels, concentrations, and intensities of prayer. I can remember praying for our middle son to live when he was in the hospital plagued with spinal meningitis and the medical team at the renown Babies and Children's Hospital in Cleveland, Ohio said that the outcome of the next thirty-five hours would be the determining factor. I can honestly say that I had never prayed like that before and never after until I went on a twenty-one-day fast when I prayed for a blessing of healing for our grandson. Prior to the twenty-one days, I could not remember to pray constantly for him. I would get so caught up in the "busy-ness" of the workday that I would not remember to pray for him until the end of the day. But while I was fasting, I prayed for him much more often. Fasting and praying brings new meaning to praying without ceasing. God did heal our grandson, and we give God all the praise and glory.

A Closer Walk with God

Simply put, fasting brings us into a closer communion with God. When we fast, we take God with us wherever we go. Fasting brings new meaning of us to the name "Emmanuel," which is "God with us." We claim we are excited about the meaning of the name Emmanuel, but our behavior indicates otherwise. An analogy can be drawn to teenagers when they ask their parents for use of the family car. Imagine the look on the teenager's face when they discover the parent is sitting in the back seat of the car when it is time to leave. Certainly the teenager did not expect the parent to be with them. Likewise, we ask God for a blessing, but we really don't want God to go or be with us. We want to say and do things that we prefer God not hear or see. Obviously, God is with us. But when we fast, we become conscious and highly aware that He is with us. If we want a closer walk with

Him, we will be obedient to His voice and make a commitment to fast and pray. God says that when we fast and pray, He will bless us openly. The blessing of just being closer to Him should be sufficient, but God, who is in the blessing business, chooses to bless us so that others can see how blessed we are in Him.

A Season of Fasting

Because Jesus is not with us in the flesh, this is a season for fasting. In Matthew's gospel the question was asked of Jesus, *"Why do we and the Pharisees fast oft, but thy disciples fast not? And Jesus said unto them, Can the children of the bridechamber mourn, as long as the bridegroom is with them? but the days will come, when the bridegroom shall be taken from them, and then shall they fast"* (Matthew 9:14,15 - KJV). This is the day, this is the time, now is the season for fasting. Jesus was crucified, buried and has risen, and is now sitting at the right hand of God the Father. He will come again to judge the living and the dead. He has left with us His person, in Spirit, to comfort us and help us. Fasting brings us closer to God by helping us walk in the Spirit and not in the flesh. When we fast, we become more conscious of the presence of His Spirit and power in us. Until His eminent return this is the season of fasting.

What Is Fasting?

From biblical examples we can determine that fasting is abstaining from solid foods for a period of time for spiritual purposes. Fasting is not dieting. Although fasting is for spiritual purposes, we must prepare physically and spiritually to fast. The very core of fasting and praying is repentance. Unconfessed sin will hinder the blessing promised for fasting and praying. We must prepare ourselves to fast by repenting and confessing our sins before God.

Without hesitation, I advise that if there are predispositions to medical problems or existing ones, fasting should only be considered after consultation with a licensed physician. Since the basic tenet of fasting rests in the denial of flesh to get closer to God for the glory of God, persons with medical restrictions can find other methods of fasting rather than abstaining from nourishment. When flesh is denied, God is glorified. There are many types of

When flesh is denied, God is glorified.

fasts and various methods of fasting. God is concerned about our motives for fasting rather than our methods.

Doing Right Wrong

God tells us we can do the right thing for the wrong reasons and lose our reward. We must be careful of the motives that inspire our religious behavior. It is possible for flesh to glorify itself through a religious act like fasting and praying. This is God's warning to us that when we fast and pray, we should not bring attention to ourselves. We should not fall in love with the religious act. We should not brag about it, for it is to God and God alone that we fast and pray. Fasting and praying can become hypocritical. God says that fasting and praying can become empty, long, self-glorifying and self-deceptive. It is indeed possible to do right wrong.

Fasting and Praying—A Christian Duty

Fasting and praying is not an option for the believer. God says, "when" you fast and pray, not "if" you fast and pray. The assumption is that it is something we must do. Fasting and praying are not spiritual gifts. Spiritual gifts help us help others get closer to God. Praying and fasting are spiritual admonishments.

Spiritual admonishments help us get closer to God. Fasting and praying are Christian duties. All believers are to fast and pray. Remember, God is in the blessing business so He does not admonish us to do something without the promise of a reward. God says that when we fast and pray, we should do it in secret and He will reward us.

A Good Time to Fast

As alluded to earlier, God does not tell us when or how often to fast. However, there are some good times to fast. First, it is a good time to fast when we need special power. God has promised such power if the believer fasts and prays. *"Howbeit this kind goeth not out but by prayer and fasting"* (Matthew 17:21 - KJV). *"And he said unto them, This kind can come forth by nothing, but by prayer and fasting"* (Mark 9:29 - KJV).

Second, there are times when we need to humble ourselves before God and become totally dependent upon Him. *"But as for me, when they were sick, my clothing was sackcloth: I humbled my soul with fasting; and my prayer returned into mine own bosom"* (Psalm 35:13 - KJV).

Third, it is a good time to fast when a special need arises, such as the need for a blessing of healing.

During these times, no food, or responsibilities should interfere with seeking the very presence of God.

Fourth, it is a good time to fast when we sense a calling on our lives, such as to the mission field or to the ministry. Fasting enhances our spirit of discernment.

Fifth, it is a good time to fast when we need deliverance. Just as it is impossible to pray and worry simultaneously, it is difficult to fast and willfully sin.

God Sees Our Needs and Our Motives

Remember, God is all-seeing and all-knowing. God knows our needs even before we ask. When we fast and pray, God not only hears our prayers, but He also sees our needs. The scripture says that the God who "sees," not hears, us in secret will reward us. He not only hears our cry, but He sees our tears.

He also sees our hearts and knows our motives. He knows if we are fasting before men or before Him. He knows if we are fasting to lose weight or to get closer to Him. We must take heed to the conditions of the promise if we want to be blessed.

The Reward (Blessing)

We are blessed in many ways through fasting and praying. Ultimately, we are blessed by our closeness to

Him. However, there are other benefits that can be counted as blessings. First, fasting keeps us in the presence of God. It is a blessing to seek His face. Second, fasting helps us stay physically fit. God wants a prepared fit vessel. Third, fasting keeps us from being in bondage to bad habits like eating late at night, or having an addiction to desserts or chocolate. Fourth, fasting keeps us disciplined and in control of ourselves. God needs disciplined learners and followers He can call disciples. Fifth, fasting helps us demonstrate our love and seriousness to God. Loving God is the first Commandment. Sixth, fasting humbles us and teaches us to be dependent on God. And seventh, fasting helps us be obedient. Obedience is the key to receiving all of the promised blessings of God. We are indeed blessed through fasting as it relates to praying.

Summary

Fasting as it relates to praying, for the most part, is an undiscovered spiritual phenomenon that is a potential blessing-bombshell ready to explode. God has promised that if we pray right and fast right, he will reward us. A challenge and formula was suggested to give the reader an opportunity to stand on this promise. Praying right and fasting does not involve seeking the approval of men for our religious acts, but rather, seeking only to glorify God. Fasting allows us to get closer to God which in itself is a blessing. Praying and fasting are not optional to the believer—it is a Christian duty to fast and pray. Because God is not with us in the flesh, this is the season for fasting. Although God does not tell us when or how often we should fast, there are some good, best, and most helpful times to fast. And when we fast, God sees our needs and our motives. We should be careful how we perform religious acts because it is possible to do good things for the wrong reasons. However, God has promised that when we fast and pray according to His Word, He will reward us. There are many benefits to fasting coupled with praying, including the ultimate blessing of obedience, which is the key to receiving all of the promised blessings of God.

Finding Favor With God and Man

Favor in Hebrew comes from the same word as the word grace. Simply put, favor is a function of God's grace. We cannot find favor with God or man without experiencing the unmerited grace of God. Throughout the Bible, God desires to favor us. However, just as we grow in grace, we must grow in favor.

The Gospel writer, Luke, tells us that *"Jesus increased in wisdom and stature, and in favour with God and man"* (Luke 2:52 - KJV). Jesus ultimately is our example and model. We ought always want to be more and more like Him. If Jesus increased in favor with God and man, we ought to as well. An Old Testament text,

283

How to Be Blessed

Proverbs 3:1–13, and a gospel lesson, Luke 2:41–52, will serve as the instructional instruments for this epilogue. With every instruction comes a promise of what's going to happen afterwards.

Proverbs 3:1–13 (KJV)

1 My son, forget not my law; but let thine heart keep my commandments:

2 For length of days, and long life, and peace, shall they add to thee.

3 Let not mercy and truth forsake thee: bind them about thy neck; write them upon the table of thine heart:

4 So shalt thou find favour and good understanding in the sight of God and man.

5 Trust in the LORD with all thine heart; and lean not unto thine own understanding.

6 In all thy ways acknowledge him, and he shall direct thy paths.

7 Be not wise in thine own eyes: fear the LORD, and depart from evil.

8 It shall be health to thy navel, and marrow to thy bones.

9 Honour the LORD with thy substance, and with the firstfruits of all thine increase:

10 So shall thy barns be filled with plenty, and thy presses shall burst out with new wine.

11 My son, despise not the chastening of the LORD; neither be weary of his correction:

12 For whom the LORD loveth he correcteth; even as a father the son in whom he delighteth.

13 Happy is the man that findeth wisdom, and the man that getteth understanding.

Luke 2:41–52 (KJV)

41 Now his parents went to Jerusalem every year at the feast of the passover.

42 And when he was twelve years old, they went up to Jerusalem after the custom of the feast.

43 And when they had fulfilled the days, as they returned, the child Jesus tarried behind in Jerusalem; and Joseph and his mother knew not of it.

44 But they, supposing him to have been in the company, went a day's journey; and they sought him among their kinsfolk and acquaintance.

45 And when they found him not, they turned back again to Jerusalem, seeking him.

46 And it came to pass, that after three days they found him in the temple, sitting in the midst of the doctors, both hearing them, and asking them questions.

47 And all that heard him were astonished at his understanding and answers.

48 And when they saw him, they were amazed: and his mother said unto him, Son, why hast thou thus dealt with us? behold, thy father and I have sought thee sorrowing.

49 And he said unto them, How is it that ye sought me? wist ye not that I must be about my Father's business?

50 And they understood not the saying which he spake unto them.

51 And he went down with them, and came to Nazareth, and was subject unto them: but his mother kept all these sayings in her heart.

52 And Jesus increased in wisdom and stature, and in favour with God and man.

Let Your Heart Be a Treasure Chest

God is trying to teach us how to be blessed by finding wisdom, understanding, and favor with God and man. First, He says that we must make our hearts treasures of godly principles. Our hearts are to be treasure chests. He tells us to have the law and the commandments hidden in our hearts. Our hearts should be treasure chests of good and godly principles and precepts.

When we have a treasure chest, we can reach down and pull something out of it. We can't pull out what's not in there. If mercy's in there, we can pull out some mercy. If truth is in there, and if His law is in there, then it's available. What He's saying here is to let our hearts be treasure chests of His commandments, of His laws, of His mercy, of His justice, of His grace, and of His truth. When we do this, we're going to find favor with God and man.

Lean Not on Your Own Understanding

Second, we are taught to lean not on our own understanding. That's probably the most familiar scripture in the Old Testament, *"Lean not on your own understanding."* Many believers know this verse of scripture, but we *still* lean on our own understanding.

Very seldom do we really seek God's will and God's guidance.

How do I know God's will? All I have to do is just find out what my will is. I know His will is just the opposite. It's simple. God is so much higher than I am and so much more powerful. If I get in touch with some of my fleshly desires, God's will draws me back to Him. So if I don't do what I want to do, I'm probably in God's will.

It's practical when He says to lean not on our own understanding. The marvelous thing is that the promise of God and favor that comes afterwards really tell us there's healing in trusting God. Scripture says that it shall be health to thy navel and marrow to thy bones. In other words, leaning not on our own understanding, trusting God, acknowledging Him in all our ways, and allowing Him to guide our path are going to bring about healing to our very essence. Our navel is the center of all we are. When we read the translation, it says, "Will be sewn up." In other words, the very essence of all that we are that is broken apart shall be sewn up, and there will be marrow in our bones. Marrow gives us the living strength of our bones.

If we have no marrow in our bones, then we have dry bones and that's what Ezekiel had in the valley. He was in the valley of "no-marrow bones." He was in the valley of dry bones, and sometimes the Christian and the church are in the valley of dry bones. Yes, we have strength to go to work, but our bones are dry, and we need marrow in our bones. He says, "Here's how you get it. Let Me give you that healing. Let Me show you what real healing is all about. Healing is trusting in the Lord. I will sew up your fragmented pieces, and I'll put strength in your bones." How do we find favor with God and man? Make our hearts our treasure chests and lean not on our own understanding.

Consecrate Your Substance

Third, we must consecrate our substance. In other words, honor God with our substance and the firstfruits of our increase. If we get a raise, we have to honor Him with that increase. We have to honor Him with the substance that we have, even before the increase. Honor Him with thy substance and the firstfruits of thine increase. And what will He do for us? Scripture says our barns shall be filled, pressed down and running over.

The Rejection of Correction

The problem many of us have is what I call the rejection of correction. Look at verses 11 and 12. *"My son, despise not the chastening of the Lord; neither be weary of his correction: for whom the Lord loveth he correcteth; even as a father the son in whom he delighteth."*

God corrects us so He can bless us with favor. But we have grown weary in our hearing. He is sending us a word of correction, but we are rejecting it because we really don't want to hear it. If we want to find favor, we can't grow weary in correction.

Why does the Lord correct us? Because He loves us. Why does the Lord correct us? Because He wants to bless us. We're not to grow weary. Many of us have raised children. We know how it is when we correct our children. Sometimes they don't want to hear it. But as children of our heavenly Father, when we hear a word of correction, we're really kind of the same way. We have learned to have more of a poker-face. We just sit there and say, "He isn't talking to me." God has a word of correction for us. He has a word of instruction for us. He's saying to us, "Make your hearts treasure chests of My precepts; lean not on your own understanding; honor Me with the firstfruits of thy substance and thine increase, and I will bless you by allowing you to have favor with God and man."

We may have fallen on hard times and we're wondering what's going on. It may be just God and His correction mode. You see, God loves us. So sometimes when we begin to stray, He has to correct us, and sometimes He even has to punish us. I'm so glad that He loved me enough to correct me, to chastise me, and even punish me. If we love our children, we will correct them. And because God loves us, He corrects us.

God wants us to find favor with Him and man by grabbing wisdom and understanding. How do we do that? First, make our hearts treasure chests of His principles; second, lean not on our own understanding; and third, honor Him with thy substance and the firstfruits of thy increase, and we will grow as Jesus grew.

Grow as Jesus Grew in Favor with God and Man

Jesus is always our model. Jesus is always our prime example. He is our hero. He is the One that we ought to follow. In Luke 2:41–52, Jesus with His parents went up to Jerusalem to the Passover. They had gone to the Passover because they were going to celebrate what God had done. People always need to celebrate what God has done. God had brought them out of slavery, across the Red Sea, so now every year they go to Jerusalem to celebrate. After the Passover, they were on their way home to Nazareth and Joseph and Mary realize that their twelve-year-old son is missing. Can you imagine? Your child is missing? They go back to inquire where He might be. Can you see them searching through the crowd as they go? They're going back through the crowd. "Has anybody seen my boy? Has anybody seen Jesus? Has anybody seen my boy? He's missing. He's not with us." And where do they find Him? They found Him in the temple, teaching and listening even to the elders. They were amazed at His wisdom even at that young age. His parents asked Him why He had not been with them, why He had stayed behind and stepped away from the crowd. His very simple answer was, "Don't you know I must be about My Father's business?" And then the Bible says He went with them and was subject unto them and grew in stature and favor in the sight of God and man. If we're going to grow as Jesus grew, we cannot follow the crowd. Jesus had to step away from the crowd. Some of us are crowd-pleasers. If we are going to find favor with God and man, we cannot be amongst the crowd. We have to step away and march to a beat of a different drummer.

Second, if we are going to grow as Jesus grew, we have to be about our Father's business. Many of us have everybody's business on our mind except our Father's business. We can't mind our own business so we can't see about the Father's business. Our capacity has some limitations. We can't have everybody else's business on our mind and be about our Father's business too. If we could mind our own business and be about the Father's business, we'd be all right. But we have programmed our minds—these computers that God has given us to store stuff—with somebody else's business. We have a search engine, and we go out there looking for other folks' business. Jesus was about His Father's business. He grew in favor in the sight of God and man because He did not follow the crowd and He was about His Father's business.

Finally, He was subject unto Joseph and Mary. If we're going to grow as Jesus grew, we must have a spirit of submission. When He returned home, He was subject. Jesus minded His parents. Jesus minded His earthly parents although He stepped from the crowd and was about His Father's business. Jesus grew up in the home of Joseph, a carpenter, and Mary. He had a submissive spirit.

There is no better favor than God's favor. As we grow as Jesus grew and as we grow in wisdom and understanding, God has promised that we will grow in His favor and in the favor of man. God's favor is the greatest thing in the world. God's favor will actually make men bless us. God's favor will make our enemies our footstool. There's love and healing in God's favor. There's joy and peace in God's favor. There's wisdom and understanding in God's favor. There's hope in God's favor. There are blessings in God's favor. There's blessed happiness in God's favor.

Summary

God's grace is not only sufficient for salvation, but it also overflows into God's blessing-ocean and causes us to be able to find favor with God and man.

God wants us to find favor with Him and man by obtaining wisdom and understanding. How? First, by making our hearts treasure chests of His principles and standards. Second, by leaning not on our own understanding, and third, by consecrating our substance by honoring Him with the first fruit of our increase.

The major reason many of us do not find favor with God and man is that we reject correction from God. God corrects us so He can bless us, but we reject His correction.

Ultimately we are to grow in wisdom and understanding and find favor with God and man as Jesus did. How? First, by stepping away from the crowd and marching to the beat of a different drummer. Second, by being about our Father's business and minding our own business. And third, by having a submissive spirit, even as Jesus was submissive to His earthly father and mother, and of course His and our Heavenly Father.